CW00455682

Mt St Michel • St Malo • Jersey • Weymouth • Poole • Cherbourg

PETIT TOUR DE
MANCHE

petit tour
DE MANCHE

petit tour DE MANCHE
Cross-Channel cycling route

1st Edition
By Mark Porter

Accommodation, Food & Drink
History, Route and Maps
In Dorset, Brittany, Normandy and Jersey.

By Mark Porter
Design: Hillside Creative
Copyright: Baytree Press ©

Published by:
Baytree Press, Primrose Cottage,
Wester Ulston, Jedburgh TD8 6TF

+44(0) 7767893790
info@cycle-guides.co.uk
www.cycle-guides.co.uk

ISBN: 978-0-9555082-8-8

📷 Many of the photographs used in the Dorset chapter were by Tim Pestridge, to whom we are extremely grateful. Tim has a tremendous eye and is one of the best recorders of life in South West England. **www.timpestridge.co.uk**

Thanks also to George Porter whose help in every department was invaluable.

CONTENTS

INTRODUCTION

Q: What have Weymouth, Poole, Cherbourg and Saint-Malo got in common?

A: Quite apart from being splendid ports, they are all staging posts on a new and exciting cycle ride that takes you, ship-to-shore, in a perfect circle.

The Petit Tour de Manche, as it's called, links the World Heritage site of Dorset with the beauty and tranquillity of North West France, forming a circular ride of around 440km. That's about 275 miles, a challenging but doable distance over a very long weekend. If you include Jersey, that makes it 505km, or 315 miles.

But to linger over it is much more fun, taking in the Channel Islands and Le Mont-St-Michel, that fabulous architectural volcano that explodes out of the sands of the Normandy coastline.

The PTM, for short, takes you from the ancient and scenic port of Weymouth and over the Ridgeway to the county town of Dorchester, before heading east through the quiet lanes of rural Dorset, where the modern world is another country.

The route wends its way gently towards the Saxon town of Wareham, then across Purbeck to Swanage and Poole, over heathland and heights, beaches and woods, to the ferry terminal to France, Jersey and Guernsey. The longest section of the ride is in France, along the Cherbourg peninsula close to the D-Day beaches, the villages and market towns of the Calvados, Manche and Ile-et-Vilaine areas, to Avranches, Le Mont-St-Michel and along the Brittany coast. You will pass the great oyster beds of Cancale and the fishing villages of the Emerald Coast. Names to conjure with, places to dawdle through.

This guide aims to help the dawdler and the challenge rider alike. It cherry-picks all that's best along the way: the best tables to dine at; cycle-friendly accommodation and good watering holes as well as lots of background information to the communities you will pass through.

PTM is one of three routes being launched by Cycle West, whose Brussels-funded remit – via the EU Interreg Channel IV Manche programme – is to broaden cultural horizons and open up the countryside of England and France's western peninsulas. For those who want an even bigger challenge, there is another route: the Tour de Manche, which takes in Devon and Cornwall plus the Breton coast as far west as Roscoff. This is a big beast of a ride (1200km or 750miles), but that's for another day...

Technical

Difficulty: easy to moderate.
The route is mostly flat and along quiet country lanes and cycle tracks. There are a few climbs in Purbeck.

 What bike?

We've devised the route to be as inclusive as possible. There are options better suited to mountain bikes, hybrids and tourers, but you can easily do the whole route on a road bike. There are always options allowing for roads or good cycle tracks for those who don't wish to take their road bikes through the elements, but winter tyres will safely see you across the roughest section, even over Rempstone in Dorset if you are happy to push for short sections.

Touring bike
Much like a road bike, except sturdier and capable of carrying panniers. They come with drop handlebars and mudguards so you don't get (quite so) covered in mud. The wheels are wider and stronger and the tyres less inclined to puncture.

The touring bike will also have a wider spread of gears than a road bike, which is very handy on the hillier sections.

Road bike
Great for roads as skinny wheels make for fast riding. But they are not so good on traffic-free, and hopeless for off-road. They are not designed to carry panniers, the double front chain ring means they are hard to take up steep inclines and they are more prone to punctures and buckled front wheels. Also, you get much muddier, as no self-respecting road bike would sport mudguards.

Having said that, you can blast across nearly all of the PTM on a road bike and if time is of the essence then simply get some good all-season tyres (Continental Grand Prix 4 Seasons came out top in a recent road test, closely followed by Michelin Pro Optimum) and these will get you over the greenways (voies vertes) with little problem.

Mountain bike

Great, up to a point. Great for those stunning but very small sections of off-road, but are they worth the hassle? I am inclined to say no, as the fat wheels make for much harder work. They have smaller wheels, much higher rolling resistance and are awkward to put panniers on. But if that's all you've got, then go for it: you can always swap the huge knobbly tyres for smooth ones.

Hybrid

A cross between a tourer and a mountain bike, these are ideal for the PTM. However my vote would be for a tourer. Every time.

Trousers

Lycra with gel pads are probably best. But you can also get baggy shorts with padding. Not everyone likes (or suits) lycra so there are options worth looking at online. You can wear ordinary shorts, but you would be well advised to get a padded liner to wear underneath, unless your posterior is seriously saddle hardy.

Tops

It is important that your body can breathe and that the sweat you will quickly generate should be able to wick. This is why a merino wool or polyester base layer is so much better than cotton, which will leave you wet and probably cold. The weather can change pretty rapidly at any time of the year, so it's a good idea to have a medium layer – for instance, fleece. Then you will need a reflective, light-weight weather-proof outer garment for those inevitable moments when the needle plunges and the heavens open.

Remember: brightly coloured, reflective tops are best. Not all drivers are as alert as cyclists!

Gloves

Fingerless are good for more moderate conditions. Gloves also protect the hands from chafing and offer padded protection if you fall.

Helmets

A must, though not legally enforceable. Get one as light as possible, so you are hardly aware you are wearing it. You can spend a fortune, but you don't need to.

Shoes

SPD pedals and trainers which clip in make for the most efficient pedalling power. They make much more sense than the cleats used by road riders as you can also walk quite normally in them. If this is beyond your budget, then old-fashioned toe-clips will do.

ITINERARIES:

There are any number of ways of dividing the route. Here we suggest just a few, starting with a crazy itinerary which will appeal mostly to masochists and road munchers.

The Monster Challenge
2 days (missing out Jersey)

DAY 1 Dorset to St-Lô: 202km (126miles)
HARD CORE ONLY.
You will need to leave Weymouth in the early hours to make the 0830 crossing from Poole. This docks in Cherbourg at 1330 and will be followed by 130km (80m) of slog, starting with a climb out of Cherbourg. Don't expect to make St-Lô until around 2000.

DAY 2 St-Lô to Saint-Malo: 234.5km (147miles)
Doable, but what a shame to have it all go by in a blur. Hard-core cyclists will manage this.

The Challenge
4 days (missing out Jersey)

DAY 1 Dorset – Weymouth to Poole 73.6km (46miles). Owing to the ferry services departing at 0830 you will most likely want to stay in Poole for the first night, unless leaving in the early hours to ensure a same-day crossing (see Monster Challenge). For hard core only.

DAY 2 Cherbourg to St-Lô – 128km (80miles). This will take at least 6 hours, but bear in mind you will be arriving in Cherbourg at 1330 so won't make St-Lô until around 2000, assuming all goes well.

DAY 3 St-Lô to Pontorson or Mont-Saint-Michel – 174km (108miles).

DAY 4 Pontorson to Saint Malo – 62km (39m).
If you get to Saint Malo you can leap on the lunch-time ferry and be back in Weymouth early evening.

The Five Day Flyer

DAY 1 Dorset – Weymouth to Poole – 73.6km (46miles).

DAY 2 Cherbourg to Carentan – 80km (50miles).

DAY 3 Carentan to Vire – 113.4km (70miles)

DAY 4 Vire to Pontorson/Mont-Saint-Michel - 108km (68miles)

DAY 5 Pontorson/Mont-Saint-Michel to Saint-Malo – 62km (39miles)

2 ferries (lunch time, via Guernsey and teatime, via Jersey) back to Weymouth.

Six Days

DAY 1 Dorset – Weymouth to Poole – 73.6km (46miles).

DAY 2 Cherbourg to Carentan – 80km (50miles).

DAY 3 Carentan to Vire – 113.4km (70miles)

DAY 4 Vire to Pontorson/Mont-Saint-Michel – 108km (68miles)

DAY 5 Pontorson/Mont-Saint-Michel to Saint Malo – 62km (39miles). Ferry to Jersey departs 1730.

DAY 6 Jersey – 65km (40.6 miles) Ferry back to Weymouth 1845.

Seven Days

DAY 1 Dorset – Weymouth to Poole – 73.6km (46miles).

DAY 2 Cherbourg to Bricquebec – 27.9km (17.5miles).

DAY 3 Bricquebec to St-Lô – 99.3km (62miles)

DAY 4 St-Lô to Vire – 65km (41miles)

DAY 5 Vire to Ducey – 76.3km (47.5miles)

DAY 6 Ducey to Saint Malo – 93.5km (59miles). Overnight Saint Malo or Jersey. This gives the option of a 60km circuit of Jersey.

DAY 7 Sail to Weymouth from either Saint Malo or Jersey.

Eight Days

DAY 1 Dorset – Weymouth to Poole – 73.6km (46miles).

DAY 2 Cherbourg to Bricquebec – 27.9km (17.5miles).

DAY 3 Bricquebec to St-Lô – 99.3km (62miles)

DAY 4 St-Lô to Vire – 65km (41miles)

DAY 5 Vire to St-Hilaire-du-Harcouët 57.3km (36miles)

DAY 6 St-Hilaire-du-Harcouët to Cancale 96.4km (60.5miles)

DAY 7 Cancale to Saint Malo 15.6km (10miles) Overnight Saint Malo or Jersey. This gives the option of a 65km circuit of Jersey.

DAY 8 Sail to Weymouth from either Saint Malo or Jersey.

Ten Days

DAY 1 & 2 crossing Dorset to get to Poole. Stop at Wareham, Corfe or Swanage. 73.6km (46miles).

DAY 3 Cherbourg to St-Sauveur-le-Vicomte – 41.6km (26miles).

DAY 4 St-Sauveur-le-Vicomte to St-Lô – 85km (53.1miles).

DAY 5 St-Lô to Sourdeval – 89.3km (55.8miles).

DAY 6 Sourdeval to Ducey – 52.1km (32.57mv).

DAY 7 Ducey to St-Benoît-des-Ondes – 66.7km (41.7miles).

DAY 8 St-Benoît-des-Ondes to Saint Malo – 26.7km (16.7miles).

DAY 9 Jersey – 65km (40.6miles)

DAY 10 Sail to Weymouth.

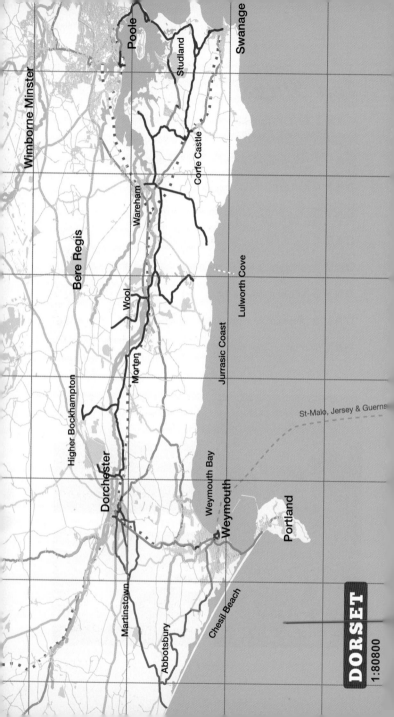

DORSET   73.9km (46.6miles)

Weymouth > Dorchester = 17.2km (10.8miles)
Dorchester > Wool = 16.7km (10.5miles)
Wool > Corfe Castle = 17.7km (11.1miles)
Corfe Castle > Poole = 22km (13.8miles)

 **Challenge:**

Intermediate with some fairly good uphills, particularly if you take the Abbotsbury loop. Purbeck hilly in places. Also a decent climb over the Ridgeway, between Weymouth and Dorchester. Otherwise, easy.

Parking

If you want to park cheaply at someone's home this is the place to look: **www.parkatmyhouse.com.** There are quite a few operators, charging as little as £3.50 per day, many of them near the ferry terminal.

Otherwise, the most exhaustive listings can be found at dorsetforyou. com/traveldorset.

Swannery car park, Radipole Park Drive, DT4 7TZ. One week deal: £38. £9.50 a day in the summer; £7.50 out of season.

Condor Ferries: 01202 207207. If you are taking the ferry you qualify for a parking slot.

Weymouth Mount Pleasant Park and Ride Mercery Road, Weymouth, Dorset DT3 5HJ. **01305 221020**.

There is also parking on Portland at the following establishments if you spend the first night:
• The Venue Hotel (Southwell Park, Portland, DT5 2NA. **01305 826060**
• The Heights, Yeates Road, Portland, DT5 2EN. **01305 821361**

For a more exhaustive list please try visitweymouth.co.uk or phone 01305 785747.

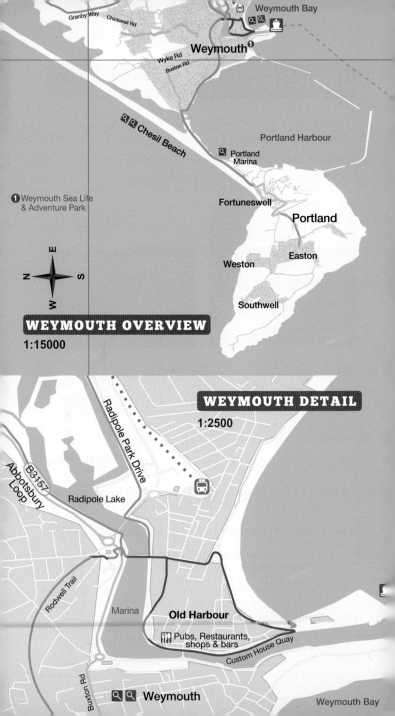

Granby Way Chickerell Rd

Weymouth Bay

Weymouth

Wyke Rd
Buxton Rd

Chesil Beach

Portland Harbour

Portland
Marina

1 Weymouth Sea Life
& Adventure Park

Fortuneswell

Portland

E
N   S
W

Easton

Weston

Southwell

WEYMOUTH OVERVIEW

1:15000

Radipole Park Drive

WEYMOUTH DETAIL

1:2500

Abbotsbury Loop
B3157

Radipole Lake

Rodwell Trail

Marina

Old Harbour

Pubs, Restaurants,
shops & bars

Custom House Quay

Buxton Rd

Weymouth

Weymouth Bay

Bike shops/hire near the start

Mudsweatandgears: Weymouth, 8 Granby Court, Granby Industrial Estate, Weymouth, DT4 9X. **01305 784849. mudsweatngears.co.uk**. Andy Leach will pick up and deliver bikes along the entire Dorset stretch.

Portland Bike Hire. 07783 456749. portlandbikehire.com. Will deliver bikes to your point of departure.

Signpost Cycling – organised holidays, Weymouth. **01305 832512. www.signpostcycling.co.uk.**

Westham Cycles, Weymouth. **01305 776977.www.westhamcycles.com**

WEYMOUTH

If Weymouth is a great point of departure, it is an even better point of return. If you've still got the energy, it's bristling with bars and restaurants, hotels and nightlife. Of course, you may wish, to use the naval term for fun, to have a good 'run ashore' before setting off.

One of the most striking and elegant sea fronts in Britain, if not Europe, Weymouth was where King George III spent 14 consecutive summer holidays from 1789. He was the foremost user of that new-fangled device, the bathing machine. This was a cart towed into the water in which bathers changed before taking the plunge. It was considered impolite to disport ones body in public, even when covered from knee to throat in bathing costume.

The port was one of the first modern 'tourist destinations', thanks to 'Mad' King George. Much of the old world charm is still there: the 18th century esplanade terraces are perfectly preserved and decorated to preserve their uniformity, even when they are rival businesses. The swagger is still evident on the quayside. Bustling pubs stand side by side, touting for your trade.

 # GETTING TO WEYMOUTH

By Train

South West Trains

South West Trains can take you to Weymouth in less than 3 hours from London Waterloo. There are 2 trains an hour and you can get a ticket from £13 if you book in advance. Visit southwesttrains.co.uk to book your ticket or call 0845 6000 650

First Great Western offers a regular daily train service from Bristol, Bath, Yeovil and Dorchester. Visit firstgreatwestern.co.uk, or call 08457 000 125.

National Rail Enquiries can advise you on how best to reach a destination. nationalrail.co.uk or call 08457 484 950.

By Coach

National Express

For times, fares or additional information, please call: 08717 818181 or www.nationalexpress.com

By Road

From the **west A38** from Cornwall & Devon, the A35 from Honiton and the A354 from Dorchester.

From the **east M3** from London & M25, M27 from Southampton, A31 from M27, A35 from Bere Regis and then A354 to Weymouth & Portland

From the **north M6** from the north, M5 from the Midlands & Wales. Weymouth is signposted from Junction 25

By Ferry

Brittany Ferries

Daily ferry service between Poole & Cherbourg. Visit www.brittany-ferries.co.uk for further information or call 0871 244 0744.

Condor Ferries

St-Malo and Weymouth via Jersey. Visit www.condorferries.co.uk for further information or call 0845 609 1024.

By Air

Bournemouth International Airport

Regular flights from: Alderney, Algarve, Alicante, Dublin, Frankfurt-Hahn, Majorca or Tenerife. Visit www.bournemouthairport.com for further information or call 0845 478 6714.

Exeter Airport

Regular flights from: Belfast, Dublin, Guernsey & Jersey. Visit www.exeter-airport.co.uk for further information or call 01392 367433.

Bristol Airport

Regular flights from: Aberdeen, Amsterdam, Brussels, Nice, Edinburgh, Belfast, Dublin, Cork, Munich and many other European destinations. Visit www.bristolairport.co.uk for further information or call 0871 334 4444.

BAA Southampton Airport

Regular flights from many European & Worldwide destinations. Visit www.southamptonairport.com or call 0870 040 0009.

Heathrow Airport

Regular flights from many European & worldwide destinations. heathrowairport.com

Where to eat? - a sample of what's on offer

Crab House Cafe, The Fleet Oyster Farm, Ferryman's Way, Portland Road, Wyke Regis, DT4 9YU **01305 788867 crabhousecafe.co.uk**. Splendid seafood shack down by the Portland causeway. 4km from town centre on NCN 26 Rodwell Trail.

Floods, 19 Custom House Quay, Weymouth, DT4 8BG. **01305 772270**. Harbourside seafood. Popular and highly rated.

Vaughans, 7 Custom House Quay, Weymouth, Dorset. DT4 8BE. **01305 769004. vaughansbistro.co.uk**. Handsome harbourside setting.

Marlboro Fish & Chips, 46 St Thomas Street. **01305 785700**. Upmarket, tempura, deep fried mackerel as well as cod'n chips.

Galley Bistro, Hope Square, Weymouth, DT4 8TR. 0**1305 784059. thegalleybistro.co.uk**. Open all year round, with open air dining in the summer. Seafood, steaks, and local beers.

The Blue Fish, Chiswell, Portland DT5 1AN. **01305 822991. thebluefishrestaurant.com**. More seafood plus interesting meat dishes down on Chesil Beach.

Quiddles Cafe, The Esplanade, Chesil Cove, DT5 1LN. **01305 820651**. Seafood shack almost in the sea. Informal café style.

Weymouth and Portland National Sailing Academy, Osprey Quay, Portland DT5 1SA. **01305 866000 www.wpnsa.org.uk**. Hosted sailing events for the 2012 Olympics. Cafe and bike parking. Team GB train here.

 Where to stay?

£ Fosters Guest House, 3 Lennox St, Weymouth, DT4 7HB. **01305 771685, www.fostersguesthouse.co.uk**.

£ Morven House, 2 Westerhall Road, Weymouth, DT4 7SZ. **01305 785075, www.morvenweymouth.co.uk**.

£ Oaklands, 1 Glendinning Ave, Weymouth, DT4 7QF. **01305 767081, www.oaklands-guesthouse.co.uk**.

£ £ Chandlers Hotel, The Chandlers B&B Guest House, 4 Westerhall Road, Weymouth, DT4 7SZ.
01305 771341. www.chandlershotel.com.

£ Acqua Beach Hotel, 131 The Esplanade, Weymouth, Dorset, DT4 7EY. **01305 776900 Mob: 07834 597339**. Comfortable and great value. Handy for station, ferry and town centre.

£ £ The Heights, Yeates Road Portland, Dorset DT5 2EN.
01305 821361. www.heightshotel.com.

£ £ The Venue, The Venue Hotel, Southwell Park, Portland, Dorset, DT5 2NA. **01305 826 060**

£ £ £ B+B Weymouth, 68 The Esplanade, Weymouth, Dorset, DT4 7AA. **01305 761190**. **bb-weymouth.com**.4-star and cycle friendly, they even offer free cycles to guests.

♡ **£ £ £ Moonfleet Manor House**, Fleet Road, Weymouth, Dorset DT3 4ED. **01305 786948.**

 ## Where to drink?

The Ship, Custom House Quay, DT4 8BE. **01305 773879**. Good food and drink on the quayside.

The Boot, High St West, DT4 8JH. **01305 770327**. 14th century pub near harbour.

Red Lion, 4 Hope St, DT4 8TR. **01305 786940**. Big outside seating area. Near harbourside.

Wellington Arms, St. Alban Street, DT4 8PY. **01305 786963**. Old fashioned back street pub.

Sailors Return, 1 St Nicholas Street, Weymouth DT4 7UF. **01305 773377**. Does B&B as well as foaming pints and pub grub.

The Old Ship, 7 The Ridgeway, Upwey, Weymouth, DT3 5QQ **01305 812522**. Four miles from centre, in northern suburbs. Good pub with good food.

The Cove House Inn, 91 Chiswell, Portland, Dorset DT5 1AW. Spectacular spot just over the causeway with great sunsets over Chesil and Lyme Bay. **01305 820895, thecovehouseinn.co.uk.**

A37
Poundbury
Damers Rd

A35
Maiden Castle Rd

Routes from
Abbotsbury
Loop

Maiden Castle
Iron Age Fort

Monkton Hill

Dorset Ridgeway

Broadwey

Littlemoor Rd

Littlemoor

Granby Way

Weymouth

Abbotsbury Rd

Rodwell

Wyke Rd

Buxton Rd

Wyke Regis

Portland Harbour

**WEYMOUTH TO
DORCHESTER**

1:6000

WEYMOUTH
TO
DORCHESTER

17.2km (10.8m)
nearly all traffic-free

Challenge:

Easy to intermediate – some
uphill over the Ridgeway. Along
roads & cycleways.

Route Info

● The ferry port is the official
start point. This makes good
sense as nearly all of you will
be returning to it from St-Malo,
on the Condor ferry. There is
also reasonably priced parking
nearby, including Condor's own
car park.

● The official route now heads
along the splendid Esplanade
taking you round to Westham
Road and over the bridge. The
other route is possibly more
splendid, following Custom
House Quay and Weymouth
Bay harbour. The water and
the moored yachts and fishing
boats should be on your left.
Custom House Quay becomes
Commercial Road. You will start
to see signs for National Cycle
Network (NCN) 26, following
the side of Radipole Lake.
There are also PTM and GTM
logos now added.

▶ Follow NCN26 on the traffic-free cycle path alongside Radipole
Lake. NCN26 then merges onto the road (Radipole Park Drive)
for a short distance. Following the signs, turn left onto Spa
Road then next right onto Icen Road, left again onto Roman
Road then right at the top of the hill onto Mount Pleasant
Avenue South which merges into a traffic-free path. Following
the NCN26 signs, cross Dorchester Road and then follow
the clearly signed path which climbs over the Ridgeway and
Dorchester beyond.

NB just outside Dorchester you will need to cross the A35. At the risk of
sounding unnecessarily nanny-like, watch out. This is a fast traffic island
on a trunk road and is not a pleasure to cross, with motorists looking
out for themselves rather than you. Those wishing to peruse this historic
town centre should follow the cycle track past the Tesco superstore
before turning right onto Sawmills Lane and on to South Court Avenue
(still part of the route). At the T-junction go left and then first right into
Manor Road which you should follow until its junction with South Court
Avenue. Here you head right, up to the traffic island. A left turn up
Culliford Road, past the Baker's Arms, takes you into the town centre;
a right turn onto Lucetta Lane takes you east, and out of town into rural
Wessex.

To Dorchester from Portland, via Weymouth (22.5km,14m)

If you decide to set off from Portland, then follow the cycle track alongside Portland Beach Road (the A354). As you rejoin the mainland just beyond the Ferrybridge Inn look out for the Rodwell Trail, which follows the old Weymouth to Portland Railway for two and a quarter miles until you are almost in the town centre. There are four old stations and halts plus a tunnel, all of which conjure up the essence of a line which closed to passengers 60 years ago. This route will link in with NCN 26 just after you cross the harbour on Westham Road.

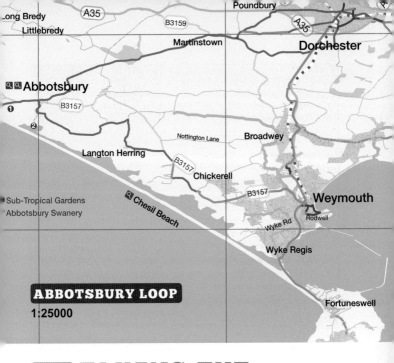

TAKING THE ABBOTSBURY LOOP

43km (27miles)   Highly recommended

Challenge:

Intermediate – climb out of Abbotsbury hardest on the whole route.
Mostly on quiet lanes.

Route Info

Those who want a real flavour of West Dorset should go from
Weymouth to Dorchester via Abbotsbury, and forget about the direct
route alongside the main road. Abbotsbury is one of England's most
perfect villages and also happens to be close to Chesil Beach, an
iconic coastal strip which has the Olympics to thank for its new,
worldwide fame.

▶ From Westham Bridge at the northern end of Weymouth Marina, follow the cyclepath along the west bank of Radipole Lake (signed Southill). The cyclepath emerges at Chafey's roundabout, which you should cross on the two southern arms to pick up the cycle track on the southern side of Granby Way (B3157).

▶ Continue due west on the Granby Way cycle track, passing a roundabout and a junction with traffic lights. The second junction – with pedestrian crossing – is a crossroads, where you should go straight across into Fleet Lane. Soon you bear right, running parallel with the coast. Go past East Fleet Farm, continuing straight on up the hill *ignoring the no-entry signs* - this is actually a bridleway. You may have to open a gate to continue. Where the bridleway joins Fleet Lane head west towards the hamlet of Fleet, passing a pretty chapel on your right. Follow Fleet Road uphill, taking the farmost right turn at the junction with Sea Barn Farm and passing West Fleet Farm on your left and heading North. This is an easyenough bit of traffic free even for a road bike with skinny tyres.

▶ Soon you're at the junction with the B3157. Go left for less than 1km and take the next left up to Langton Herring and Rodden, where a sharp left will bring you onto the lane that will, in about 5km, take you into Abbotsbury.

ABBOTSBURY

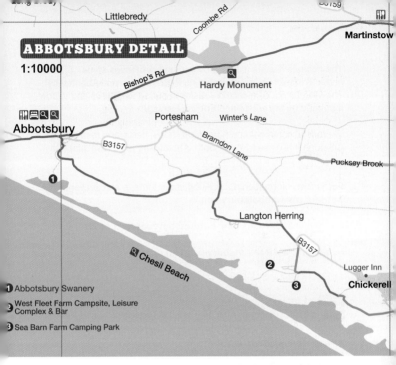

ABBOTSBURY DETAIL

1:10000

Abbotsbury

B3157

Littlebredy

Coombe Rd

Martinstow

Bishop's Rd

Hardy Monument

Portesham   Winter's Lane

Bramdon Lane

Pucksey Brook

Langton Herring

B3157

Chesil Beach

Lugger Inn

Chickerell

❶ Abbotsbury Swanery

❷ West Fleet Farm Campsite, Leisure
Complex & Bar

❸ Sea Barn Farm Camping Park

Many of the buildings here are medieval, dating back more than
500 years, and are built from honey-coloured Jurassic limestone.
Abbotsbury is known for its Swannery and Sub-Tropical Gardens.
The Swannery is the only managed nesting colony of mute swans
in the world, and was originally established by monks as a source of
fresh meat for the banquets at St Peter's monastery. This was a fine
ecclesiastical site founded by King Canute for the Benedictines in
the 11th century, but destroyed 500 years later by Henry VIII during
the Dissolution of the Monasteries.

The reeds that grow in the Fleet - that long stretch of brackish
lagoon between Chesil Beach and the landmass of Dorset - provide
an ideal habitat for nesting swans. The area has been inhabited
since just after the last Ice Age, and there are some 20 ancient
burial chambers (tumuli) nearby, attesting to its popularity as a
settlement since long before the Saxons and Vikings.

The Ilchester Estate is family owned and comprises some 15,000 acres (61 km2) of Dorset, including Chesil Beach and Abbotsbury. The village was painstakingly restored during the 1970s and is now managed by the estate and English Heritage.

There is accommodation here, plus shops, cafes and restaurants. Although it is close to Weymouth, Abbotsbury is an ideal place to stay if you want a real flavour of the Chesil Beach area.

For further information about Abbotsbury there is an excellent website: **www.abbotsbury.co.uk.**

Sub-tropical gardens: **www.abbotsburygardens.co.uk**

Swannery: **www.abbotsbury-tourism.co.uk.**

 ## Where to sleep?

Abbey House, Church St
01305 871330 www.theabbeyhouse.co.uk

Linton Cottage, Rodden Row
01305 871339 www.lintoncottage.co.uk

Ilchester Arms Hotel, Market St
01305 871243 www.ilchesterarms.co.uk

 ## Where to eat?

Abbotsbury Tearooms
26 Rodden Row
01305 871143

Ilchester Arms Hotel
Market St
01305 871243
www.ilchesterarms.co.uk

Route Info

▶ At the Ilchester Arms go left if you first want to visit Chesil Beach. Having come this far, it would be a shame not to. Or go right, up Back Street towards the Hardy Monument. This is the toughest bit of the PTM coming up, so be warned. You climb from sea level to 240 metres in the space of 6km if coming from Chesil Beach, but only one stretch is likely to have you pushing (especially if you're kitted out with saddlebags).

✱ Chesil Beach

The shingle beach stretches for 18 miles (29km) from Portland to West Bay and is around 200 metres wide and 15 metres high. Between the beach and mainland Dorset is a tidal lagoon, the Fleet, which is a haven for birdlife. The beach and the Fleet form part of the Jurassic Coast, a UNESCO World Heritage site.

▶ After about 3km you will come to a cross-roads, where you will meet up with NCN2/Tour de Manche route, the east to west national cycle route connecting Kent with Cornwall. If you fancy exploring further into West Dorset, take a left and head into the rural tranquility of deepest Wessex, through such villages as Littlebredy, Litton Cheney and Loders before you get to the great market town of Bridport. Well worth a visit, Bridport is one of the liveliest towns in Dorset, with some great places to eat, sleep and drink.

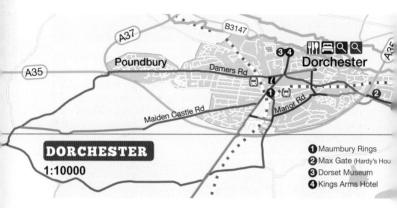

DORCHESTER

1:10000

1 Maumbury Rings
2 Max Gate (Hardy's Hou
3 Dorset Museum
4 Kings Arms Hotel

If you're continuing to Dorchester, go straight on at the crossroads, taking the Tour de Manche and NCN 2 signs, eastwards. You will pass the village of Portesham (down in the valley to the right), where another famous Thomas Hardy once lived. You can still see the eagles on the gate to his house. Once you are past Hardy's monument, it is an easy ride into Dorchester. The monument, by the way, has nothing to do with Thomas Hardy the writer: it is in memory of Thomas 'Kiss Me' Hardy, the naval admiral to whom Lord Nelson uttered his final, deathless words, having been mortally wounded at the Battle of Trafalgar. It is a National Trust property and you can climb the tower for great views. Take care on the steep descent!

Carry on through Martinstown, taking the lane to the left, which comes immediately at the end of the village. If you're on a road bike you should continue down the lane, ignoring the NCN 2 traffic-free route through Clandon Farm on the right. Go to the end of the lane, as far as the A35 traffic island, where you take a right along the B3150 into the centre of Dorchester, where you link up again with NCN 2.

Other cyclists may wish to do the traffic-free option across occasionally muddy bridleway, taking you past the ancient burial grounds at Clandon Barrows and Maiden Castle.

 Where to drink?

The Brewers Arms, Martinstown, Nr Dorchester, DT2 9LB. **0844 683 5087**. Former girls' school put to a new use in 1865. Food and drink.

DORCHESTER

An elegant Georgian county town, Dorchester began life as an Iron Age hill fort at Maiden Castle, which was on your right if you took the Abbotsbury loop, or on your left if you came straight from Weymouth. Tribes first existed here 4,000 years ago, ruling the strategic area until the Romans defeated them 2,000 years later, in 70AD. Parts of the Roman walls are still in evidence today and the town has stayed on the same site ever since, a regional market town for two millennia.

After the Saxons came the Vikings, but in the 17th century Dorchester became a centre of Puritanism. At that time many of the Pilgrim Fathers who settled on America's east coast gathered in Dorchester before setting sail.

An anti-Royalist stronghold during the Civil War, later the rebellious spirit produced the Tolpuddle Martyrs (1833). Seven farmworkers provided the foundations for the trade union movement by swearing an oath of allegiance to the Friendly Society of Agricultural Labourers. The Martyrs were condemned to transportation to Australia for their pains. The government backed down, however, when the masses who marched on London were able to brandish a petition signed by 800,000 people.

At the town's western gate lies Poundbury, a Duchy of Cornwall urban village idea, still half way in the making. This is a 25 year project to 'implement the principles' expounded in the Prince of Wales's 1989 book, 'A Vision of Britain.' Its curious profile is prominent from the ring road, giving it a slightly futuristic fairytale look, suggesting a modern-medieval fusion. The Prince's futuristic vision is due for completion in 2025.

 ## Worth seeing

Dorset County Museum, High St West, DT1 1XA
01305 262735
www.dorsetcountymuseum.org

Max Gate, Thomas Hardy's house, Alington Avenue, DT1 2AB, **01297 489 481**

Thomas Hardy It is testament to how great a writer Thomas Hardy was that this whole area – Wessex – is synonymous with his work. The novelist and poet, who loved cycling the leafy lanes of Dorset, was born just outside Dorchester and spent most of his long life there. The town is the setting for two of his best known novels, The Mayor of Casterbridge and Tess of the d'Urbervilles (Dorchester is Casterbridge).

Thomas Hardy's Cottage, Higher Bockhampton, near Dorchester DT2 8QJ. Hardy's Birthplace. **01305 262 366**

Thomas Hardy's Cottage

 Where to sleep?

♡ **£/££** **Westwood House**, 29 High West St. **01305 268018**

££ **The King's Arms Hotel**, High East St. **01305 265353**

££ **The Old Ship Inn**, High West St **+44(0)1305 264455**

£££/£ **The Casterbridge Hotel** 49 High East St. **01305 264043**

£££/£ **Wessex Royale Hotel**, 32 High West St. **01305 262660**

Baytree House, 4 Athelstan, Dorchester, DT1 1NR. **01305 263696 www.bandbdorchester.co.uk.** They have secure bike storage and already host cyclists

Beggars Knapp, Weymouth Avenue, Dorchester DT1 1QS. **01305 268191 www.beggarsknap.co.uk.**

Aquila Heights, 44 Maiden Castle Road, Dorchester, DT1 2ES **01305 267145 www.aquilaheights.co.uk.** Secure bike lock up.

Bramlies, 107 Bridport Road, Dorchester, DT1 2NH. **01305 265778 www.bramlies.co.uk.** Cyclists welcome.

31

Where to eat?

Sienna, 36 High St West, Dorchester DT1 1UP. **01305 250022. www.siennarestaurant.co.uk**. High-class modern British cuisine in a pocket-sized location.

The Horse with The Red Umbrella (tearoom), 10 West Street, Dorcester, DT1 1UJ. **0844 683 5208**. Oak beamed tearoom on the high street.
No 6, 6 North Square, Dorchester, DT1 1HY. **01305 267 679**. Seafood. The French chef likes the taste of Mediterranean sunshine.

La Caverna, 57 Icen Way, Dorchester, DT1 1EW. **0844 683 8203**. Family run Italian.

Dorset Kitchen, 22-23 South Street, Dorchester, DT1 1DA. **0844 683 8197**. Been in business for 110 years inside Goulds department store.

 ## Where to drink?

The Blue Raddle, 9 Church Street, Dorchester, Dorset, DT1 1JN. **01305 267762**. Old-fashioned, charming real ale pub.

Tom Browns, 47 High E St Dorchester, Dorset DT1 1HU **01305 264020**. Basic pub serving variety of beers.

Bakers Arms, 140 Monmouth Road, Dorchester, Dorset, DT1 2DH. Well liked town centre freehouse.

 ## Bike Shops

Dorchester cycles
31 Great western road, DT1 1UF Dorchester, **01305 268787 dorchestercycles.co.uk. sales@dorchestercycles.co.uk.**

DORCHESTER TO WOOL

16.7km (10.5miles)

Challenge: Easy. Country lanes.

Route Info

This is easy and scenic cycling, rolling countryside, wood and pastureland, and thatched cottages. From the Lucetta Lane roundabout head east to the end of Lucetta Lane where a short stretch of traffic-free cycleway links with Balmoral Crescent and Alington Avenue and Came View Road. The whole section from Came View Road to the West Stafford turn-off is traffic-free. The track takes you to the outskirts of West Stafford via a minor road. Carry on through the hamlets and villages of West Woodsford and Woodsford, Moreton, East Burton, East Stoke and Wool, following signs clearly marked NCN 2 & PTM.

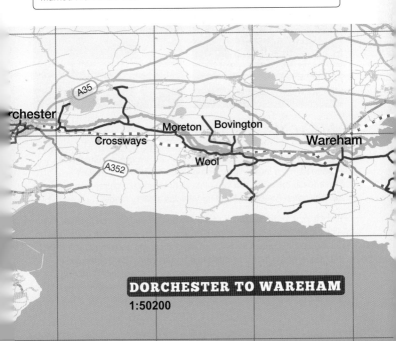

DORCHESTER TO WAREHAM
1:50200

MORETON

A great place to stop off for refreshments are the multi-award-winning Moreton Tea Rooms, where you can sit outside on those occasionally sunny summer days. Just across the road, near the River Frome, is the churchyard where T.E. Lawrence (better known as Lawrence of Arabia), was buried after his untimely motor cycle accident in 1935. He rented Clouds Hill cottage while serving at Bovington Camp.

♡ **Moreton Tea Rooms**, The Old School Moreton, Dorchester DT2 8RH. **01929 463647.**

WOOL

Half-way between Dorchester and Wareham, Wool is a hamlet that expanded into a large village owing to the considerable military presence in the area. You can often hear the distant crump and boom of the Bovington Armoured Fighting Vehicles artillery range.

Wool is at a fordable stretch of the Frome and you will see the old bridge – no longer in use for vehicles. It is about 200 metres north of the station and has an inscription stating that anyone caught defacing or damaging the bridge would be transported to a penal colony. Beside the river is Woolbridge Manor, a 17th century manor that was the 'Wellbridge House' of Hardy's 'Tess of the D'Urbervilles', where she spent her doomed honeymoon.

WOOL TO WAREHAM

Challenge: Easy.

9.6km (6miles)

Route Info

▶ Cross the railway line at the level crossing and turn immediately left and continue staight on with the station on your left then take the first left. Follows minor road, again picking up NCN 2 & PTM signs. Woodlands, farmland and open scrub.

WAREHAM

Definitely worth a look. Overnight, if you have the time. 1km off the route. At Stoborough instead of turning right onto Nutcrack Lane head northwards on the B3075 across the floodplain and you will see Wareham ahead of you.

An elegant Georgian town centre with visible roots that go back to the Saxon times of King Alfred the Great. Wareham lies between the rivers Frome and Piddle, at the head of the Wareham Channel of Poole Harbour. Its strategic position first appealed to *homo sapiens* as long ago as 9000BC, when Mesolithic settlers first dug flint pits. Inhabited throughout the Bronze Age, the remnants of a 3,500 year old house were recently uncovered here.

The earth ramparts surrounding the town date back to the 9th century and were built by King Alfred as a defence against the Vikings. There are two churches with Saxon origins – Lady St Mary and St Martins-on-the-Wall. However much of the medieval architecture was destroyed in a fire in 1762 and the subsequent rebuild explains the striking Georgian appearance.

Like Bruges, Wareham owes its spectacular preservation to silt: both towns ceased to be major trading ports as a result of water channels becoming clogged with sand. They became towns that time left still and Wareham is really worth a visit. The Tourist Information Centre, housed in a spectacular 14th century former church, has all the details: Holy Trinity Church, South Street, Wareham, Dorset BH20 4LU. 01929 552740.

Worth seeing

Wareham Town Museum, Town Hall, 3 East St Wareham BH20 4NN. **01929 553448**. Wtm.org.uk. tells the story of the area from prehistoric times. It has a special section on Lawrence of Arabia and is regularly updated with new exhibits. Run by volunteers.

The Quayside. Sit outside at one of the pubs and soak up the ancient atmosphere.

Boat hire: Abbot's Quay, Wareham. **01929 550688.** **warehamboathire.co.uk.**

 Where to eat?

The Old Granary, The Quay, Wareham, BH20 4LP. **0844 683 8234**. Well run bistro/pub on the banks of the Frome.

The Quay Inn, The Quay, Wareham, BH20 4LP. **0844 683 8237**. Outside seating. Good pub grub.

Monsoon Indian Cuisine, Northport, Wareham, BH20 4AT. **0844 683 8276**. Good family run curry house near the station.

 Where to drink?

Kings Arms, 3 Corfe Road, Stoborough, Wareham, Dorset, BH20 5AB **01929 552705 www.thekingsarms-stoborough.co.uk**

The Duke of Wellington, 7 East St, Wareham BH20 4NN. **01929 553015**. Traditional real ale pub.

The Horse and Groom, St Johns Hill, Wareham BH20 4LZ. **01929 552995**. Friendly and good value. Highly rated locally.

The Red Lion, North Street, Wareham, Dorset, BH20 4AB. **01929 550099**. Good value food and real ale.

The Old Granary, The Quay, Wareham BH20 4LP. **0844 683 8234**. Well run bistro/pub on the banks of the Frome.

The Quay Inn, The Quay, Wareham BH20 4LP. **0844 683 8237**. Outside drinking. Great setting.

Where to sleep?

€ Hyde Cottage, 48 Furzebrook Road, Stoborough, Wareham **01929 553344.**

€ Holmebridge House, Wareham **01929 550599.**

€€ Gold Court House, St John's Hill, Wareham. **01929 553320.**

€€ The Red Lion, North Street, Wareham. **01929 550099.**

♡ **€€€€ Priory**, Church Garden. Wareham. **01929 551666.**

Springfield Country Hotel, Grange Road, Wareham. **01929 552177. thespringfield.co.uk. enquiries@thespringfield.co.uk**

WAREHAM TO CORFE CASTLE

10.4km (6.5 miles)

 *Challenge:* Intermediate. Quiet lanes. Busy road just before Corfe Castle. Be warned!

Route Info

▶ Recross the Frome, heading along the South Causeway back to Stoborough. Immediately beyond the King's Arms, go left down Nutcrack Lane. At the crossroads go straight across to Arne Rd, taking the second turning on the right after about 2.5km, continuing to follow NCN2 & PTM (or you can go straight on to visit the RSPB bird sanctuary overlooking the Wytch Channel at Arne). Keep following the NCN signs until you arrive at the busy A351, which you follow for about 1km before arriving at Corfe Castle.

▶ This should only be tackled by experienced cyclists. Instead, why not jump aboard the steam train at Norden Park & Ride and get a lift into Corfe (bikes are taken for free) **dorsetforyou.com/396460** and **swanagerailway.co.uk/n-stations.htm**.

▶ **Off-road via Rempstone Heath:** For those who want to go more directly to the Shell Bay ferry terminus to Sandbanks and Poole,

> ● missing out Corfe Castle and Swanage, then you can take the alternative off-road NCN2/PTM route across Rempstone Heath along the old tramway. For this, take a left turn about 2.5km from where you turned off Arne Road. It is clearly marked, but you will need to keep your eyes open.
>
> ● After about 8km of splendid heathland, with great views of the rolling Purbeck Hills, you will find yourself on the road down to the ferry (sign-posted sharp left). Poole harbour begins to open up.
>
> ● The Rempstone Ride is a spectacular cross-country route – fine for touring bikes and mountain bikes, but not advisable on a road bike.

CORFE CASTLE

This is one of England's prettiest villages, nestling under the striking ruins of the castle. Corfe Castle itself was built just after the Norman Conquest and stood proud until it was partially demolished in 1646 by Cromwell's men during the Civil War. William the Conqueror enjoyed hunting in Purbeck Forest. The village grew around the castle and was largely built during medieval times to house castle and quarry workers. It is hewn from Purbeck stone and is remarkably well preserved.

For the last 300 years or so the Castle and much of the village was in the hands of the Bankes family but in the 1980s they handed it over to the National Trust. Corfe has the smallest town hall in England, but even so there is room (just) for a museum. Well worth a look.

This is one of the most delightful stop-offs on the Petit Tour de Manche, boasting some fine pubs and small hotels.

Worth seeing

Next to the Victorian railway station is **Swanage Railway Museum**, in the restored Goods Shed. Full of artefacts from the London and South Western Railway and Southern Railways.

Town Museum (in the town hall) and Model Village (at the entrance to the castle).

 ## Where to eat & drink?

National Trust Tea Rooms, The Square, Corfe Castle BH20 5EZ. **01929 481332**. Traditional Dorset cream teas and food.

Bankes Arms, Corfe Castle, Dorset, BH20 5ED. **01929 480206 www. bankesarmscorfe.co.uk.** A great pub with a garden that backs onto the Swanage Steam Train line.

Mortons House, East St, Corfe Castle BH20 5EE. **01929 480988. mortonshouse.co.uk.** Fine dining.

Model Village Courtyard Café, The Square, Corfe Castle BH20 5EZ. **01929 481234. corfecastlemodelvillage.co.uk.** Hefty Dorset cream teas plus light meals.

The Fox Inn, West Street, Corfe Castle BH20 5EE. **01929 480449. foxinncorfe.co.uk.**

The Castle Inn, East Street, Corfe Castle BH20 5EE. **01929 480208. castleinncorfe.com.**

The Greyhound Inn, The Square, Corfe Castle BH20 5EZ. **01929 480205. greyhoundcorfe. co.uk**. Large garden. Modern British cuisine cooked with passion.

 **Where to sleep?**

💷💷 **Alford House B&B**, 120 East Street, Corfe Castle BH20 5EH. **01929 480156. alfordhouse.com**

💷💷 **Ammonite B&B**, 88 West Street, Corfe Castle BH20 5HE. **01929 480188. ammonite-corfecastle.co.uk**

💷💷 **Olivers B&B**, 5 West Street, Corfe Castle BH20 5HF. **01929 477111. oliversbedandbreakfast.co.uk.**

♡ 💷💷💷/💷💷💷💷 **Mortons House**, East Street, Corfe Castle BH20 5EE. **01929.480988. mortonshouse.co.uk.**

💷💷 **Bankers Arms**, The Square, BH20 5ED. **01929 480206.**

CAMPSITES

Corfe Castle camping & caravaning, Corfe Castle, BH20 5PQ. **01929 480280.**

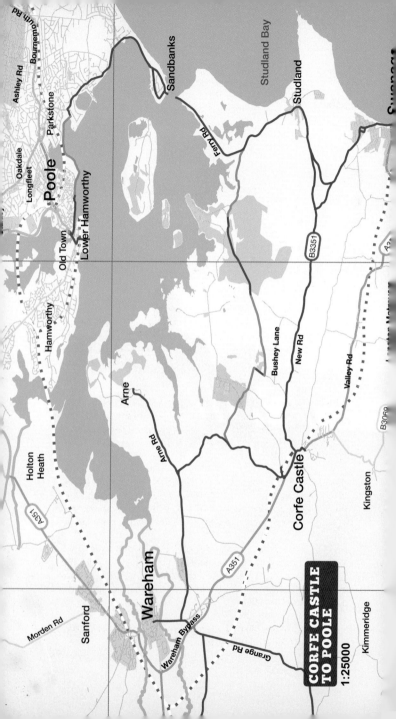

CORFE CASTLE TO POOLE

1:25000

CORFE CASTLE TO POOLE

22km (13.8 miles)

Challenge:
Intermediate.

Route Info

There are three options…

○ **(a)** From Corfe, briefly retrace your steps downhill along the A351 for 0.5km, keeping the castle on your left. As you leave the village, head right along the B3551. This road will take you all the way to the ferry, past the National Trust's Studland Beach. If you want to visit Swanage, turn right at Currendon Farm, past Ulwell and New Swanage.

○ **(b)** Alternatively, you can join the Rempstone Ride. Head up to the B3551 (as above) but take the second left turn at Ashey Copse, after about 1.5km. After less than 1km on Meadus's Lane you should turn right onto a traffic-free section of NCN2, which will take you all the way to Ferry Road.

○ **(c)** The third way, and far the easiest: board the steam train at Corfe (bikes travel free) and get off at Swanage. It's about 7km to Ferry Road, but there are a few hills. This will appeal to those who like traditional English seaside resorts, for this is one par excellence.

○ CHAIN FERRY: At the bottom of Ferry Road you will find yourself on a spit of land at the entrance to Poole Harbour, with Sandbanks just a few minutes sail away. The chain ferry runs daily every 20 mins from 0700-2310 from Studland. £1 single for cyclists and pedestrians or £3.50 for cars.

Contact: Office, Shell Bay, Studland, Swanage, Dorset, BH19 3BA
T: 01929 450203. sandbanksferry.co.uk

◗ **NB** If you are coming the other way – from Poole to Weymouth – then the recommended route from the ferry to Corfe takes you past Studland. You can ignore the B3551 and take the road on to Ulwell and New Swanage, where you head sharp right for 2.5km, before heading left at the T-junction past Herston Yards Farm and down past Herston Halt station (on the steam rail link). Turn right onto Herston High St and continue through Langton Matravers.

Just beyond is the tiny hamlet of Acton where the road splits. Take the right hand option on the B3069 through to Kingston, where you turn right down the steep hill into Corfe. Those wishing to visit the fascinating pub at Worth Matravers should hang a left instead of taking the B3069. The Square and Compass is an ancient, higgledy-piggledy affair with no bar, a small museum, home-made cider and splendid, hearty food. This adds 4km to your journey.

◗ You disembark at Sandbanks and follow the cycle lane round the bay and into Poole. This is well signed and flat, taking you past some of the most expensive real estate in the world (Sandbanks has the highest proportion of multimillionaires in Britain).
Look out for Brownsea Island

❯ THE SWANAGE LOOP

Challenge: Intermediate.

Worth seeing/doing

Swanage Railway: six miles of rail buffs' nirvana, this is a glorious throwback to the 1950s, to steam trains and holidays on the English coast. The line was not just closed, but ripped up in 1972. Since then it has been restored by the Swanage Railway Trust, section by section by volunteers. It runs from Norden Park & Ride, close to Corfe Castle. Bookings can be made online: swanagerailway.co.uk or call **01929 425800**. There's an on-train buffet and you can grab some refreshment at the stations, too.

Studland Bay: famous for its beaches (named South Beach, Middle Beach and Knoll Beach) and nature reserve. There are four golden miles of sand ideal for bathing (if you don't mind the cold), and include Britain's most popular naturist beach. Great views of Old Harry Rocks and the Isle of Wight. Run and managed by the National Trust, there are designated trails through the dunes and woodlands, which are all seething with wildlife. Studland was the children's writer Enid Blyton's inspiration for Toytown in the Noddy books.

SWANAGE

Plenty of you will wish to visit this traditional, upmarket Victorian seaside resort. Its Blue Flag beach is sheltered by Ballard Down to the north and Peveril Point in the south, while the Isle of Wight protects it against prevailing winds creating a micro-climate.

Swanage is at the heart of the Isle of Purbeck (actually, more of a peninsula than an island) and its population – 12,000 in the winter – swells to 48,000 in the summer. People flock there

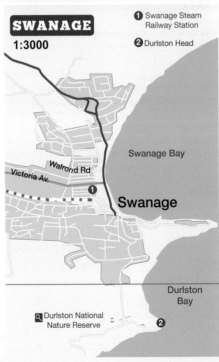

SWANAGE
1:3000

1 Swanage Steam Railway Station

2 Durlston Head

Swanage Bay

Walrond Rd
Victoria Av.
1

Swanage

Durlston Bay

🔍 Durlston National Nature Reserve

2

for the sandy beaches, dramatic cliff tops and large areas of unspoilt countryside.

The quarries of Purbeck provided the stone for St Paul's Cathedral in London as well as many other fine buildings in the capital. The stone was shipped out of Swanage on ships that returned laden with London bricks as ballast. The area of Little London was built from old London.

Swanage was a resort for the rich during the early part of the 20th century and is now home to an annual film festival, blues festival, literary festival and a host of other arty events.

Tourist Information Centre: next to the beach at Shore Road. **0870 442 0680. swanage.gov.uk.**

 Where to eat

○ **Tawny's**, 52 High Street, Swanage BH19 2NX **01929 422781. tawnyswinebar.co.uk**. Hearty and well executed dishes. Puddings a triumph, as is the wine list. Great stop off.

The Corner Restaurant, 1 Institute Road, Swanage, BH19 1BT. **01929 424969.** Seasonal menus and daily specials, local produce. Meat and fish cooked with style.

Shell Bay Seafood Restaurant, Ferry Road, Studland, nr Swanage BH19 3BA. **01929 450363**. Shellbay.net. On Purbeck island near ferry. Outside area, good bistro seafood. Cheap house wine.

Restaurant at The Grand Hotel, Burlington Road, Swanage, BH19 1LU. **01929 423353**. Stunning views across Swanage Bay and Peveril Point. House wine £9.95.

The Crows Nest Inn, 11 Ulwell Road, Swanage BH19 1LE. **01929 422651**. Good pub food and welcoming atmosphere. Popular with locals.

For the perfect picnic: The Purbeck Deli, 26 Institute St, Swanage BH19 1BX. **01929 422344**. purbeckdeli.co.uk. Top class deli: organic soup, fresh local crab baguettes. Hampers, pasties, olives…The list is long.

Where to sleep?

The Swanage Haven, 3 Victoria Road, Swanage BH19 1LY. **01929 423088**. swanagehaven.com. Run by Dave and Dianne Cole. Comfortably refurbished, licensed – Corfe brewery ales – and serves meals. Great value for money.

The White Horse, 11, High St, Swanage, Dorset, BH19 2LP. **01929422469**. Basic accommodation and good real ale.

Ocean Lodge B&B, 3 Park Road, Swanage, Dorset, BH19 2AA. **01929 422805**.

The Castleton, 1 Highcliffe Road, Swanage BH19 1LW. **01929 42397**.

Purbeck House Hotel & Louisa Lodge, 91 High Street, Swanage BH19 2LZ. **01929 422872. purbeckhousehotel.co.uk.**

The Pines Hotel, Burlington Road, Swanage BH19 1LT. **01929 425211. pineshotel.co.uk.**

Grand Hotel Swanage, Burlington Road, Swanage BH19 1LU. **01929 423353. grandhotelswanage.co.uk**

Where to drink?

The Crows Nest Inn, 11 Ulwell Road, Swanage BH19 1LE. **01929 422651**. Big, bustling and well run pub.

The Black Swan, High Street, Swanage, Dorset, BH19 2NE. Close to beach, pleasant landlady, lovely beer. Home cooked food.

The White Horse, 11, High Street, Swanage, Dorset, BH19 2LP. **01929 422469**. Solid pub grub and good real ale.

The Ship, 23a High Street, Swanage, BH19 2LR. **01929 423855**. One of the only pubs with a view of Swanage Bay. Food and fine beers.

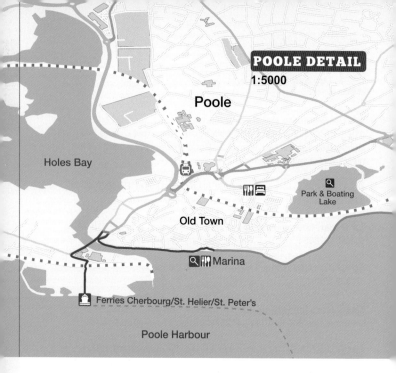

POOLE DETAIL
1:5000

Poole

Holes Bay

Park & Boating Lake

Old Town

Marina

Ferries Cherbourg/St. Helier/St. Peter's

Poole Harbour

POOLE

Poole has been described as the Kensington of Dorset – flash cars, big yachts, wealthy residents, well groomed ladies who lunch: a far cry from the rural wilderness you have just cycled through. You won't be seeing many ploughmen in the pubs of Sandbanks.

The harbour is the second biggest in the world after Sydney, though is quite shallow (the average depth is 50cm). You will have noticed its scale on the ferry and cycle route into town. Brownsea Island, seen from close up on the ferry, is the largest of eight islands in the harbour and is famous for its birdlife.

Poole's old harbour is handsome. Creaking spars of ancient trading packets vie with designer yachts and fishing boats to cast an afternoon shadow across the quayside. Here the grand mansions of sea captains and merchants still stand, fine examples of 18th century Georgian and, occasionally, medieval, architecture. Salty old pubs and trendy restaurants stand side-by-side, vying for your company. Poole is a gem of preservation, like so many of the places along the Wessex arm of this route.

One of Poole's most infamous sons was 'Arripaye' (Harry Paye), the scourge of French and Spanish shipping. He was a swashbuckling pirate, smuggler, hostage taker and privateer who caused havoc and terror along the Channel and down the Bay of Biscay. After burning down Gijon and Finisterra, a mini Armada was launched against Poole in 1405. After a fierce battle, the gallant men of Poole drove back the raiders using thick doors as shields, but not before the church and town cellars were burnt. Paye escaped but his brother was put to the sword. 'Arripaye's revenge was thorough and his antics are even now celebrated in an annual 'Paye Day' in mid-June, when piracy and pirate-speak are the order of the day.

Now a relatively safe haven for sailors, wildlife and water sports, Poole boasts Britain's best beach, Sandbanks, which was awarded more Blue Flags than any other UK resort.

And with one of the longest coast lines thanks to the 110 miles of inland harbour and sandy beaches, there is much to see and explore. To get some idea of the sheer number of great places to eat and groovy bars overlooking the waterfront, visit **eatoutpoole.com** for a more complete restaurant listing, including menus and special events.

Worth seeing

Brownsea Island: can be reached by Brownsea Island Ferries **01929 462383 brownseaislandferries.com**. Poole Quay. There is a wharf and a small dock near the main castle. The island is 2.4 km long and 1.2 km wide and consists of 200 hectares of woodland, heathland and salt marsh. Peacocks and wading birds abound and it is one of the last redoubts in southern England of the native red squirrel. nationaltrust. org.uk.

Poole Quay: you can't miss it. Take the time to stroll around and enjoy. Restaurants and bars, yachts and people-watching. poolequay.com.

Waterfront Museum, 4 High St, BH15 1BW. **01202 262600**. **poole.gov.uk/museums**. Maritime history exhibits from Iron Age longboats to the Poole flying boats in a trendy building which combines an 18th century warehouse with a contemporary glass-fronted atrium.

Bike Shops

Dorset Bike Hire
256 Sandbanks Road, Poole, BH14 8HA.
01202 708264. dorsetbikehire.co.uk

 History in a nutshell

Inhabited since the Iron Age, when the Celts moved down from the great forts at nearby Maiden Castle and Badbury, Poole was much used during the Roman occupation and later became part of the Kingdom of Wessex under the Saxons. Then in 1015 along came the Viking leader Canute the great, who used the harbour as a base for mass pillaging and plundering before launching himself upon London. Its strategic importance grew under the Normans, just as Wareham's waned. During the English Civil War in the 1640s Poole was a staunchly Parliamentarian stronghold in an otherwise Royalist Dorset, and it was from here that Cromwell's men marched to destroy Corfe Castle. The town's seafarers cornered the market in salt cod thanks to trading links with the North American colonies and, in particular, Newfoundland. Fortunes were made sailing across, filling up with salted cod and flogging the preserved fish to France, Italy and Spain, returning to harbour with salt, wine, olive oil, dried fruit and spices. This wealth explains the extravagant houses.

* For further information contact the tourist office on the quayside (0845 234 5560; **www.pooletourism.com**; Poole Quay; 10am-6pm Jul-Aug, 10am-5pm Apr-Jun & Sep-Oct, 10am-4pm Mon-Sat Nov-Mar).

GETTING TO CHERBOURG – Brittany Ferries

Daily morning sailings Poole to Cherbourg (mid-March to November) is Brittany Ferries' shortest crossing. The fastest conventional cruise ferry sailing to France is on the Barfleur, reaching Cherbourg in 4.5 hours.

Poole and Cherbourg are pleasant ports with a range of local amenities and facilities. They are easily reached with access to excellent road networks to ensure your journey is as smooth as possible.

Brittany Ferries, New Harbour Road, Poole BH15 4AJ. **0871 244 1403. brittany-ferries.co.uk.**

Bike hire
FJB Watersports Academy provides bike hire. **www.thewatersportsacademy.co.uk. 01202 708283**

 ## Where to eat?

Guildhall Tavern, 15 Market St, Poole BH15 1NB. **01202 671717. guildhalltavern.co.uk.** Converted pub in Poole's Old Town specialising in seafood. French owners and the closest you will get to authentic French dining without crossing the channel.

Patrick's, 1 Bournemouth Road, Ashley Cross, Poole BH14 0EG. **01202 734000. patricksrestaurants.co.uk.** Independent family run restaurant and bar in the heart of the lively Ashley Cross bar scene serving modern classics in the evenings and great value lunches.

Branksome Beach, Pinecliff Road, Branksome Chine, Poole BH13 6LP. **01202 767235. branksomebeach.co.uk.** Modern restaurant right on Poole's golden sands. Diners have included British chefs Marco Pierre White and Gordon Ramsay.

Harbar Bistro, Harbour Heights, 73 Haven Road, Sandbanks, Poole BH13 7LW. **01202 707272. harbourheights.com.** At the Harbour Heights Hotel, the restaurant has 2AA rosettes and the best views in town from a fantastic terrace looking over Poole Harbour.

Storm Fish Restaurant 6 High Street, Poole BH15 1BP. **01202 674970. stormfish.co.uk**. Next to Poole Quay, chef Pete 'the Prawn' Miles creates imaginative and highly rated seafood dishes.

The Bay Café, Parkstone Bay Marina, Turks Lane, **01202 724915**. This is a tiny decked wooden chalet in millionaires' row and is an oasis of calm. Cuttlefish and chorizo stew crispy haddock fishcake and a casserole of Scottish mussels cooked Belgian style by Belgian chef Stephane all come in for praise.

 ## Where to sleep?

£ The Foundry Arms, 58 Lagland Street, Poole BH15 1QG. **01202 772600. foundryarms.co.uk**. Charming and unspoilt Victorian pub. Good food and cheap rooms.

£ Mariners Guest House, 26 Sandbanks Road, Poole BH14 8AQ. **01202 247218/07983 347284. themarinersguesthouse.co.uk**. Cycle friendly. Near ferry.

£ Harlequins B & B, 134 Ringwood Road, Poole BH14 0RP. **01202 677624. harlequinsbb.co.uk.**

£ £ Corkers Restaurant & Cafe Bar with Rooms, 1 High Street, The Quay, Poole BH15 1AB. **01202 681393. corkers.co.uk**. Handy for the ferry. Comfortable and well run with a good restaurant.

£ £ Thistle Hotel, The Quay, Poole BH15 1HD. **01202 666800. thistle.com.**

£/£ Holiday Inn Express, Walking Field Lane, Poole BH15 1RZ. **01202 649222**. hiexpoole.co.uk. Handy for ferry.

£ £/£ The New Beehive Hotel, 53 Canford Drive, Cliff Cliffs, Poole BH13 7JF. **01202 701531**. thenewbeehive.co.uk. Newly refurbished and close to beaches.

£ £ £ £ The Haven Hotel, 161 Banks Road, Poole BH13 7QL. **0845 337 1550**. havenhotel.co.uk. Art Deco luxury at the tip of the Sandbanks peninsula. Next to the Studland ferry.

£ £ £ £ The Sandbanks Hotel, 15 Banks Road, Poole BH13 7PS. **0845 337 1550. sandbanks.co.uk**. Direct access onto a blue flag beach. Views across the beach and Poole Harbour.

££££ **The Harbour Heights**. 73 Haven Road, Sandbanks, Poole, Dorset BH13 7LW. **0845 337 1550. harbourheights.com**. Boutique hotel boasting a terrace with the best views of Poole Harbour.

♥ **££££** **Hotel du Vin & Bistro**, Thames Street, The Quay, Poole BH15 1JN. **01202 785570. hotelduvin.com**. Among the merchant houses in the Old Town, just off Poole Quay

 Where to drink?

The Custom House, Poole Quay, BH15 1HP. **01202 676767.** customhouse.co.uk. Part of Poole's past, now a café bar with great outdoor tables from where you can relax and pick your luxury Sunseeker motor yacht, built on the opposite side of the harbour. Good atmosphere and good restaurant upstairs.

The Cow, 58 Station Road, Poole **01202 723155**. Greene King brewery pub serving great food.

The Blue Boar, 29 Market Close, Poole BH15 1HE. **01202 682247. blueboarpoole.co.uk.** Has been in the Good Beer Guide for the last 15 years and serves good pub food.

The Angel, 28 Market St, Poole Dorset County BH15 1NF. **01202 666431**. Good locals' pub near town centre.

The Foundry Arms, 58 Lagland Street, Poole BH15 1QG. **01202 772600. foundryarms.co.uk**. Charming and unspoilt Victorian pub. Good food and cheap rooms.

♥ **Poole Arms**, The Quay, Poole, Dorset BH15 1HJ. **01202 673450.** Nice green tiled frontage. Simple but pleasant interior with nautical decor. Seafood driven menu, good Ringwood beers.

The Antelope Hotel, 8 High Street, Poole BH15 1BP . **01202 672029.** "The Antelope Hotel has a 500+ year history, 'arguably the oldest inn in Poole' claims the Antelope. Famous old coaching inn which still retains part of its original 15th century building.

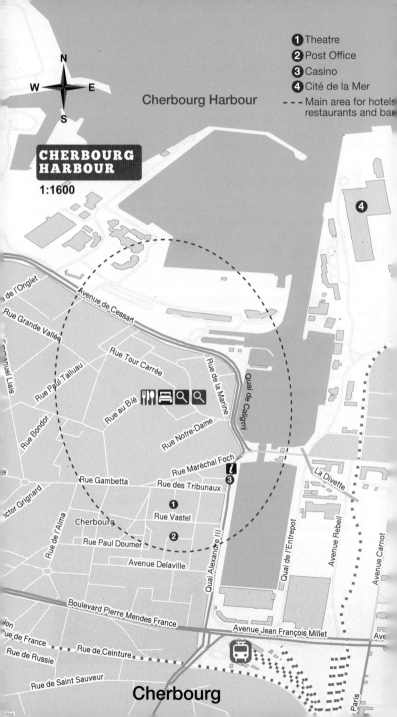

Cotentin Peninsula

COTENTIN PENINSULA 79km (46 miles)

► CHERBOURG TO CARENTAN

Challenge:

Easy to intermediate.

The route in France is on minor roads but mostly 'voie verte' or 'Greenway': those on road bikes are advised to use winter tyres as the greenways have a sand and compact gravel surface which can occasionally be loose.

Cherbourg > Brix = 15.8km (9.9miles)

Brix > Bricquebec = 12.1km (7.6miles)

Bricquebec > St-Sauvuer-le-Vicomte = 13.6km (8.5miles)

SSLV > La Haye-du-Puits = 16.1km (10miles)

LHDP > Baupte = 12.9km (8.1miles)

Baupte > Carentan = 8.6km (5miles)

NB in France, as many of you will know, there are no longer many bars outside the towns and cities. Restaurants often provide this service, so drinking is generally done over a meal. Consequently 'places to drink' have often been merged with 'places to eat'.

55

CHERBOURG

This is a fine old port that most people pass straight through. You might well opt to do this, and head into the Cotentin countryside. But if you have the time, the maze of alleyways, bustling bars and clusters of restaurants in the old town down by the quayside are well worth exploring.

This is the world's biggest artificial harbour and is still an important naval and merchant base, with a significant amount of the French arsenal securely stored here. Work on the current harbour began nearly 250 years ago and took 70 years to complete, with the harbour walls stretching for 6km. Cherbourg's proximity to England made fortifications a primary concern as the English had earlier trashed the splendid harbour built by the great engineer, Vauban, sinking half the fleet while they were at it. It was Napoleon's intention to invade England from this vast port, a plan he never got round to fulfilling.

 Worth seeing

Fort du Roule is the forbidding looking fortress which looks down on the port from the Montagne du Roule. It was originally built in the 5th century, though the current building is mostly 19th century. Standing on a rocky hill that dominates the inland skyline, Fort Roul commands a view across the entire town. Inside, there's a museum dedicated to the liberation of Cherbourg (Musée de la Libération) following the nearby D-Day landings of World War II. The Allied forces needed to capture the harbour in order to secure supplies for the liberation of Europe. It was a fierce battle fought in the early summer of 1944, made all the harder by the port's superb defences, which the Nazis had taken in 1940. The museum was expanded for the 50th anniversary of D-Day and now covers 800 sq. metres and contains 17 rooms.

The port area and the old town

Office de Tourisme, 2 Quai Alexandre III, 50100 Cherbourg-Octeville. **02 33 93 52 02. cherbourgtourisme.com**. Open all year.

La Cité de la Mer, Gare Maritime Transatlantique, 50100 Cherbourg. **02 33 20 26 26. citedelamer.com**. The top tourist attraction in Cherbourg, this is a superb and enormous maritime museum, the centre piece of which is undoubtedly Le Redoutable, France's first nuclear submarine. Longer by almost a half than a football pitch and more than 10m wide, this terrifying beast was launched by General de Gaulle in 1967. Spend an hour or so going round it and then try imagining being on board for 70 days before seeing light. There's also a reconstruction of the interior of the Titanic, which docked here on April 12 1912 before its fateful trip across the Atlantic.

COTENTIN PENINSULA

The entire Cotentin Peninsula is dotted with fine beaches renowned for their Blue Flag status water quality. The coastline is steep and rugged in parts, whilst undulating and sandy elsewhere, offering a wonderful variety. Little wonder it has proved so popular with artists. There are, of course, the D-Day beaches of Utah, Omaha, Gold, Juno and Sword plus museums and military memorabilia.

There's also a great hiking route (for another day!) along the coastline (the GR 223). It takes you past all the coves, caves, creeks and fishing villages between Mont-St-Michel and La Baie des Veys near Carentan, on the other side of the peninsula (330km).

Most of the towns you will be passing through were rendered to rubble by Allied bombs during the summer of 1944, as Operation Overlord unfolded and the Germans retreated. They have been restored – with varying degrees of aesthetic sensibility – and are lively, charming stop-offs. There's great food to be had plus some fine local cider and Calvados.

You will be passing through Asterix country. Roman and Gaulish remains have been uncovered over the years, showing evidence of bitter fighting. The area is now so tranquil that it is hard to imagine the hue and cry of war.

Where to eat?

Antidote, 31 Rue au Blé, 50100 Cherbourg. **02 33 78 01 28**. restaurant-cherbourg.fr. In the heart of the old town with a sunny terrace. Fusion French and Oriental. Good value, good standard.

Le Vauban, 22 Quai Caligny, 50100 Cherbourg. **02 33 43 10 11**. Overlooks the quayside. You can watch the kitchen in action and would be well advised to: this is seafood cooking at a high level.

Restaurant La Régence

Café de Paris, 40 Quai de Caligny, 50100 Cherbourg. **02 33 43 12 36**. restaurantcafedeparis.com. Opposite the old port with commanding views. Seafood and local produce. Superb cuisine.

Le Faitout, 25 Rue Tour Carrée, 50100 Cherbourg. **02 33 04 25 04**. restaurantlefaittout.com. Just behind the marina and decked out like a yacht, a splendid, traditional eatery.

L'Imprévu, 32 Rue Grande Rue, 50100 Cherbourg. **02 33 04 53 90**. restaurantlimprevu.free.fr. Creative menu from local produce. Does takeaways. Smack in the centre.

Le Pily, 39 Rue Grande Rue, 50100 Cherbourg. **02 33 10 19 29**. le-pily. com. Michelin-starred, classical French cooking. This is the top place in Cherbourg.

Le Plouc 2, 59 Rue au Blé, 50100 Cherbourg. **02 33 01 06 46**. Old-fashioned look, traditional style in the centre of town. Good value.

Le Pommier, 15 bis, Rue Nôtre Dame, 50100 Cherbourg. **02 33 53 54 60**. Trad cooking of a high quality at a low price. Contemporary bistro-style with a smart teak terrace.

Taï Pan, 8-10 Place de la République, 50100 Cherbourg. **02 33 93 00 81**. Cool spot to eat or just have a drink. Asian Fusion. Two terraces.

Where to sleep?

💚 💷 **Napoléon****, 14 Place de la République, 50100 Cherbourg.
02 33 93 32 32. hotel-napoleon.fr. Great situation, friendly hosts.
Terrific value. Splendid bars nearby. £ for £, unbeatable.

💚 💷 💷 Hotel **La Régence*****, Quai de Claigny, 50100 Cherbourg
02 33 43 05 16. laregence.com. Well run and attractive establishment
with a first rate restaurant. Friendly service.

💷 💷 **Marine Hotel Cherbourg Plaisance*****, Allée Président Menut,
50100 Cherbourg. **02 33 44 01 11. mercure.com.**

💷 💷 **Ambassadeur Hotel****, 22 Quai de Caligny, 50100 Cherbourg.
02 33 43 10 00. ambassadeurhotel.com.

💷 💷 **Angleterre****, 8 Rue Paul Talluau, 50100 Cherbourg.
02 33 53 70 06. hotelangleterre-fr.com.

💷 💷 **Le Louvre****, 2 Rue Henri Dunant, 50100 Cherbourg.
02 33 53 02 28. hotel-le-louvre.com.

💷 💷 **Hotel de la Renaissance****, 4 Rue de l'Eglise, 50100 Cherbourg.
02 33 43 23 90. hotel-renaissance-cherbourg.com.

TOURLAVILLE (on route)

💷 💷 **Hotel du Manoir*****, 656 Avenue des Prairies, 50110 Cherbourg.
Slight 40 year time warp effect here, but comfortable and well run,
nonetheless.

💷 **Première Classe***, 382 Rue des Pommiers, 50110 Cherbourg.
02 33 43 18 60. Basic, clean accommodation.

HOSTELS

L'Espace Temps, 33 Rue Maréchal Leclerc, 50100 Cherbourg.
02 33 78 18 78. fjt-escpacetemps.fr. Single en-suite rooms (no
doubles) 15 minutes walk from the station. €20.

Tourlaville, Centre de Collignon, Collignon, 50110 Cherbourg.
02 33 54 80 68. mairie-tourlaville.fr. En-suite rooms sleep 2 – 4. €19 - €27.50.

Glacerie, Gite de la Manufacture, Village de la Verrerie, 50470 Glacerie.
02 33 44 69 30. gitedelamanufacture.com. 4 rooms with 3 beds
(1 suitable for the disabled). €16.

Camping

La Saline**, Rue Bourgeois, 50120 Cherbourg. **02 33 93 88 33**.
equeurdreville.com. Municipal campsite 1km from the town centre,
linked by a cycleway. Water sports, spa, sauna, massage etc. €4.94 per
tent.

Tourlaville. Le Collignon***, Tourlaville. Rue des Aigues.
02 33 20 16 88. Next to the sea 3km from Cherbourg. Kayaks and
nautical outward bound activities. Swimming pool. €9 per person.

 ## Where to drink?

There are plenty of bars along the quayside. A few minutes walk away,
tucked away near the Place de la République are the following:

Le Bayou, 5 Rue Tour Carrée, 50100 Cherbourg. **02 33 53 04 55**.
Cocktail bar with terrace. Good drinking bar. Good food served, too.

 L'Eldorado, 52 Rue François Lavieille, 50100 Cherbourg.
02 33 53 08 68. Has its own brewery. A splendid beer drinkers bar.

Le Solier, 52 Rue Grande Rue, 50100 Cherbourg. **02 33 94 76 63**. Irish
bar tucked away behind the Quai Caligny.

> CHERBOURG TO BRICQUEBEC

28km (17.5 miles)

Challenge:

medium to easy. Some climbing out of Cherbourg. Mixture of quiet
roads and Greenway. Traffic-free at start and end.

Goes through: Tourlaville, Brix and Rocheville.
Cherbourg to Ravalet Château des Ravalet in Tourlaville: cycle lanes.
Tourlaville to Rocheville: minor roads with little traffic.
Rocheville to Bricquebec: Greenway – fine for all bikes, but road bikes
advised to put winter tyres on as the surface can be loose and sandy.

Route Info

The route takes you out of the busy port and onto the quiet byways of rural Normandy, climbing for a while before you are amongst the fields, meadows and orchards. At Rocheville you pick up the reclaimed rail line. Look out for the castles and fortified manor houses that dot this once battle-scarred terrain, vestiges of the Hundred Years War and other interminable tribal squabbles.

▶ Follow the multi-lane route towards the exit of the ferry port and very shortly you will see what looks like a giant zebra crossing (where the large blue warehouses on the right come to an end). Here you need to cross over, heading right, through two gates at either side of the old railway line. This takes you onto the cycleway (véloroute). You can either head left onto the route, picking up signs for Mont-Saint-Michel, alongside the Bvd Maritime. Or go right and visit Cherbourg, to have a look around the port and the Cité de la Mer, carefully retracing your steps to the port to get back en route.

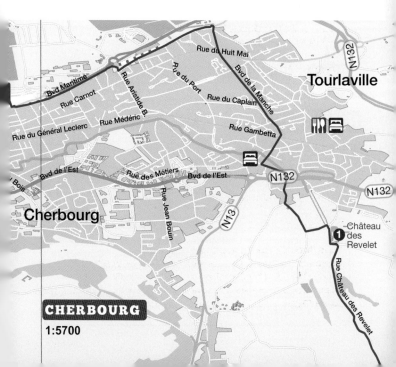

CHERBOURG

1:5700

▶ Follow the signs up to the Bvd des Flamands for about 1km before taking a right onto the Bvd de la Manche (following the cycleway), crossing the Rue Gambetta (D901) where it becomes the Bvd du Cotentin. After 300m go left onto the Rue de la Chasse à Eaux for about 100m before turning right onto a narrow pathway which takes you beside a stream under the N13. Continue along Rue des Sourds heading left up the Chasse des Picards, taking the first left and then right.

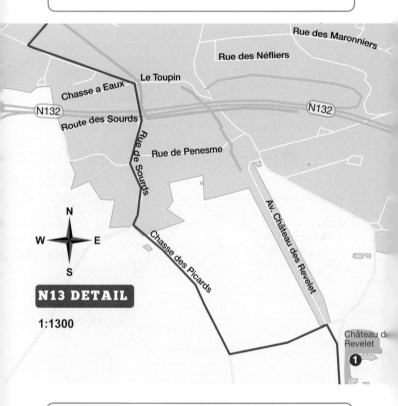

N13 DETAIL

1:1300

▶ You are now on Rue Château des Ravelet (a continuation of the D322). Don't forget to stop and admire the château. Continue for some 5km until the crossroads at the D121. Go left here.

▶ The D121 bears left and follows the N13 for some 300m before you take a quick right and left at the Route de la Verrerie, into the Route des Tuileaux. Continue until the T-junction with the Route du Mont Hébert. Go right, crossing the N13, joining the tree-lined Route du Pont d'Aumaille. After about 500m you get to a staggered crossroads, where the road dog-legs. Bear round to the right and take the first left, staying on the Rte du Pont d'Aumaille.

▶ At the junction with the D119 go left and then first right into the Route de la Rade where you bear right before going round a left-hand bend, continuing for 300m before turning left into Hameau Launay/Route du Petit Vivier, having skirted the small town of Brix.

▶ Continue for approximately 3km, to the cross-roads with the D262, taking a right (Rue des Vesques). After 1km you turn right for 25m before taking the first left. After about 1km you will hit the D418, where you bear right for 2.5km until reaching Rocheville. At the T-junction bear left for 100m and off to the right is the first section of Greenway – la Voie Verte. The lovely town of Bricquebec is only 6km away, and well worth a stop-off.

BRIX

According to legend this is where Robert the Bruce hails from. The Bruce family accompanied William the Conqueror in 1066, settling in northern England before crossing the border into Scotland. The rest, as they say, is history. Some 240 years after the Battle of Hastings, young Robert did something similar in Scotland, seizing the crown in 1306.

There's a bar, a post office and a couple of shops here, but for most it will be too early to consider stopping off.

BRICQUEBEC

This is a handsome little town with a huge market square in front of the castle ramparts. The 900 year old Château de Bricquebec and Abbaye Nôtre Dame de Grâce has a wonderful courtyard with a doorway leading from the marketplace (and car park) onto the high street. Bricquebec was originally settled by the Vikings and has witnessed a violent history, to which the castle bears scarred testament.

There are shops and bars (and even a very helpful cycle shop: **Peugeot Cycles, 27 Rue des Frères Frémine**), plus a couple of small hotels. This is indeed a tempting spot to spend a night, even though it's so close to Cherbourg.

If you do decide to overnight it here, there are two contrasting but top-notch places to rest your head.

🛏 Sleep?

💷💷/💷💷💷 At the upper end is **l'Hostellerie du Château**, Cour du Château. **02 33 52 24 49**. This is a medieval hall with a Gothic façade serving high end, traditional French cuisine.

💷 **Hotel Restaurant Le Donjon***, 2 Place Sainte-Anne, 50260 Bricquebec. **02 33 52 23 15. hotel-le-donjon.fr**. Good, no nonsense restaurant with bar. Terraced area looking across at the castle. Booking essential. Popular spot.

1 Chateau de Bricquebec
2 Hotel Restaurant Le Donjon
3 Peugeot Cycle Shop
- - - Market Place 4 car park

Bricquebec

D50

D902

BRICQUEBEC

1:1200

BRICQUEBEC TO CARENTAN

51.2km (31.1miles)

Challenge: easy. Greenway.

Bricquebec to St-Sauveur-le-Vicomte: 13.6km (8.5miles)
St-Sauveur-le-Vicomte to La Haye-du-Puits: 16.1km (10miles)
La Haye-du-Puits to Baupte: 12.9km (8.1miles)
Baupte to Carentan: 8.6km (5.4miles)

The first stage of the ride takes you to St-Sauveur-le-Vicomte (13.6km) on cycle path along the old railway line. This is a tree-lined, easy section bringing you out on the outskirts of St-Sauveur. Follow the signs past the restaurant/bar.

ST-SAUVEUR-LE-VICOMTE

1 Abbey
2 Municipal Campsite
3 Campsite
4 Chateau
- - Shops

To visit the fine castle here turn left at the roundabout, onto the Rue Raoul Hersen. The Château de Saint-Sauveur-le-Vicomte is an ancient abbey and castle dating back to the 11th and 12th centuries. It was besieged twice during the Hundred Years War between England and France, and in 1374 its walls were breached by cannon during a siege – one of the first successful uses of artillery against city walls. This happened again in 1944, but the damage was repaired in 1996.

The fortified and turreted walls surround a large keep and the castle is open to the public. The French Ministry of Culture listed it in 1840 as a 'monument historique'.

Where to sleep?

There is a municipal campsite (**02 33 41 72 04**) under the castle walls.

£ £ Auberge du Vieux Château **, 9 Avenue Division Leclerc, St-Sauveur-le-Vicomte. **02 33 41 60 15. auberge-vieux-chateau.fr.** Ivy clad, old-fashioned and comfortable old hotel right opposite the castle.

 Point of Interest

Office de Tourisme Cantonal,
Le Vieux Château, 50390, Saint-Sauveur-le-Vicomte. **02 33 21 50 44**.

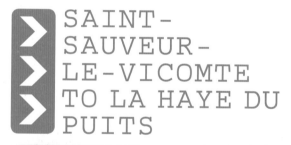

SAINT-SAUVEUR-LE-VICOMTE TO LA HAYE DU PUITS

16.1km (10.7miles)

C *Challenge:* Easy. Greenway.

Route Info

Hard to get lost, so long as you retrace your steps down the Rue Bottin Desylies and Rue Raoul Hersen back to the Greenway. And remember to turn left rather than right! The old line is pleasantly shaded by trees and takes you to La Haye-du-Puits.

Just before La Haye, on the outskirts of the hamlet of St-Symphorien-le-Valois, you have to leave the trail briefly, following PTM signs, until you relink with the Greenway. The route skirts La Haye, but if you want to pay a visit, turn right onto the Rue du Château.

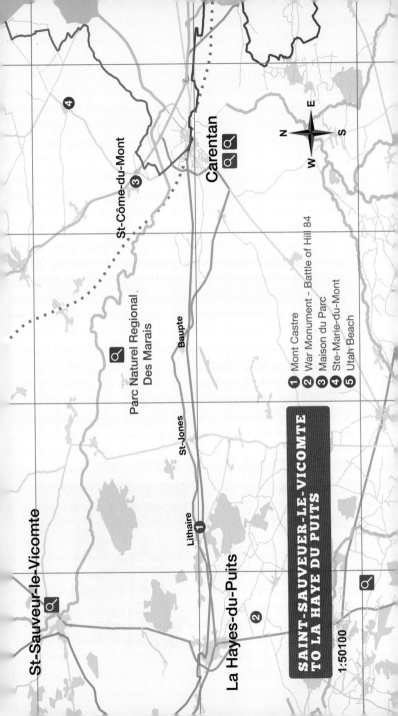

St-Sauveur-le-Vicomte

Parc Naturel Regional.
Des Marais

St-Côme-du-Mont

Carentan

Baupte

St-Jones

Lithaire

La Hayes-du-Puits

N E S W

1 Mont Castre
2 War Monument – Battle of Hill 84
3 Maison du Parc
4 Ste-Marie-du-Mont
5 Utah Beach

**SAINT-SAUVEUR-LE-VICOMTE
TO LA HAYE DU PUITS**

1:50100

Where to sleep?

Camping l'étang des haizes ****, 43 Rue de Cauticotte, Saint-Symphorien-le-Valois. **02 33 46 01 16. campingetangdeshaizes.com**.

 Point of Interest

National parkland

Between St-Sauveur and La Haye you enter the **Parc Naturel Régional des Marais du Cotentin et du Bessin** (a national nature reserve to preserve the delicate local ecosystem). This is a haven of wildlife, particularly birdlife – stretching across to Carentan, almost coast to coast, covering much of the central area of the peninsula. This marshland pulses with wildlife and used to cut off the northern Manche area, turning it into a 'presqu'île'. This vast area is still impassable in winter, save by road or Greenway. Spring and autumn bird migrations make a spectacular sight.

There are two centres well worth visiting if you are not pressed for time and are into birdlife.

Parc Naturel Régional des Marais du Cotentin et du Bessin

Siège Administratif
17 Rue de Cantepie
50500 Les Veys
Tél. **02 33 71 61 90**
Fax. 02 33 71 61 91
parc-cotentin-bessin.fr

Maison du Parc
3 Village Ponts d'Ouve
50500 Saint-Côme-du-Mont
Tél. **02 33 71 65 30**
Fax. 02 33 71 65 31
parc-cotentin-bessin.fr

LA-HAYE-DU-PUITS

Look out for the fine monument to the 5,000 Allied troops killed here during the Battle for Hill 84. The medieval cobbled town is within walking distance and has several pleasant bars and restaurants dotted around its pretty 12th century church.

LA-HAYE-DU-PUITS TO CARENTAN

21.5km (13.6miles)

e *Challenge:* Easy. Greenway.

Route Info

4km east of La-Haye is Mont Castre Castle, perched above the village of Lithaire (as you cross the D140 it is 500m to the left). This tower has kept watch over the village and the Marais de la Sangsurière since time immemorial. Prehistoric remains have been found plus evidence of scrapping between the Romans and the locals. For this is the land of Asterix, and the Gauls had ruled the roost since long before Julius Caesar tried to subdue it.

The route continues through rolling farmland and national park, past the tiny community of Baupte, which is only 5m above sea level. To the right you can make out the big peat bog – an area of land that has been returned to nature. Elsewhere the low lying wetlands make ideal pastures for dairy cattle.

Just before you get to the centre of Carentan the Greenway gives way to minor roads again, with waysigns to guide you through the town centre. Unless signage has improved there is serious scope for confusion here. The track deposits you on the Rue de la Guinguette. You bear left, keeping the railway line to your left. After around 500m take the Rue de Tolloly *under* the rail lines, turning right onto the Boulevard de Verdun

CARENTAN

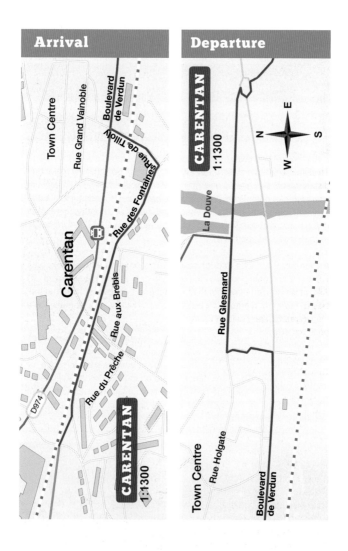

This is an ancient port, now some distance from the sea. Carentan was much fought over in 1944 as it was vital for the Allies to capture in order to link up troops at Utah and Omaha beaches. They were divided by the Douve estuary and the Germans had flooded surrounding fields. The Allies also needed a staging post before taking on German forces strongly encamped at Cherbourg and Octeville.

Now Carentan – Gateway to the Cotentin Peninsula – is a major centre for the dairy industry, with a huge cattle market. There is still some fine architecture, including the octagonal spire of the Eglise Notre-Dame, which dominates the low lying land in a similar way to Ely Cathedral in the English Fens. The covered market in the Place de la République dates from the 14th century and the author Balzac features a fine old house in the corner of the Place Guillaume-de-Cerisay in his novel Le Réquisitionnaire.

 ## Where to sleep?

£ £ **Auberge Normande**, 11 Boulevard de Verdun. **02 33 42 28 28 / 02 33 42 00 72.** **www.aubergenormande.com.** Restaurant and bar. 13 rooms.

£ £ Hôtel L'escapade 1*, 28 Avenue de la Gare. **02 33 42 02 00.** **hotelrestaurantescapade.com.** Bright and breezy looking town centre hotel with restaurant.

£ Hôtel Le Vauban, 7 Rue Sébline, 50500 Carentan. **02 33 71 00 20.** Pretty basic.

£ **Chambres d'Hôtes de la 101ème**, 26 Rue de la 101iéme Airborne, 50500 Carentan. **02 33 71 00 43. bnb-normandie.com.** Smart B&B, well run and comfortable. 5 mins walk from town centre.

There is plenty of accommodation towards Utah and Omaha beaches. If you wish to organise a further itinerary to take these centres of military pilgrimage on board you could start with looking at: **musee-memorial-omaha.com.**

The nearest to Carentan is the Musée du Débarquement Utah Beach, 50480 Sainte-Marie-du-Mont. **02 33 71 53 35. utah-beach.com.** Open every day 1000 – 1800, Oct to May (last entry no later than 1700). June to Oct open every day 0930 – 1900. Closed Dec & Jan. Entry €11 & €7. Excellent museum now with a hangar to house full size replica aircraft. This is a significant detour – at least 30km along roads.

NB If you decide to visit the war museums and beaches, be warned: the route leading up to Utah beach can get busy in the summer.

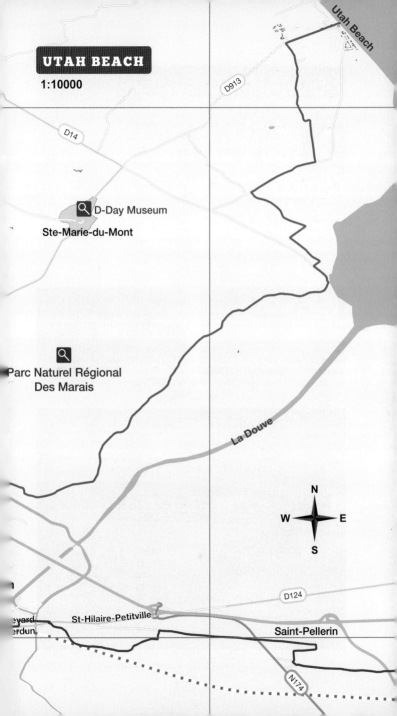

LE MARAIS
79.7km (49.8miles)

CARENTAN TO PONT FARCY

Carentan > St-Jean-de-Daye = 25.8km (15.6miles)
St-Jean-de-Daye > St-Lô- = 23.1km (14.4miles)
St-Lô > Condé-sur-Vire = 12.1km (7.6miles)
CSV > Pont Farcy= 16.1km (10miles)

Challenge:

Easy riding through varied countryside. Woodlands, riverside, shared use of lanes and Greenway.

CARENTAN TO SAINT-LÔ

48km (29.1miles)

Route Info

The next 30km or so are along shared lanes. Leaving on the Rue de Verdun, after 1km you will head right onto the Rue de la Mare which, in a couple of km, will bring you onto the D544 where you head right. Keep on the D544 for 2.5km, crossing the E3, before going right on the D89, at Saint-Pellerin.

A dog leg takes you back on yourself before bringing you out on the D544 again, the Rue de la Tranquerie, soon going over the new Route Nationale 174.

The D544 winds around a fair bit, taking you through some woodlands (you are entering the *'bocage Normand'*). You will also notice many horses grazing in the lush pastures: this is the capital of France's equestrian industry. The place is dotted with racecourses.

Soon you will skirt the small community of Monmartin-en-Graignes, turning right at the T-junction with the D444. Go up the hill out of town, crossing the traffic island (and the N174) and stay on the Route des Mésanges for about

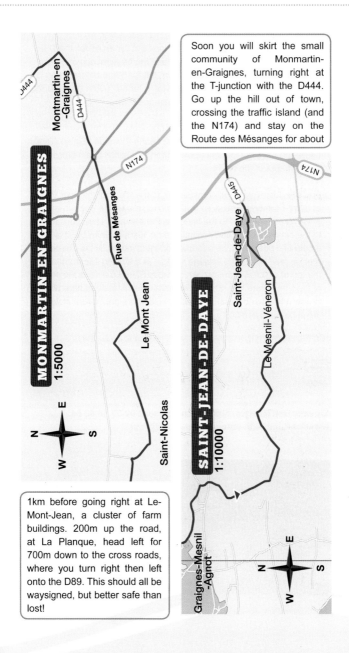

1km before going right at Le-Mont-Jean, a cluster of farm buildings. 200m up the road, at La Planque, head left for 700m down to the cross roads, where you turn right then left onto the D89. This should all be waysigned, but better safe than lost!

> Just before Graignes-Mesnil-Angot look out for signs for the D389, which skirts the centre of the village and the huge racecourse, taking you down to the D257 where you turn left for 500m before going left again for 500m. Take the first right for a further 500m down to the D445. In 4km you will be in Saint-Jean-de-Daye.

> Take the D445 down the Place de la Mairie, turning briefly right on the Rue St-Jean and immediately left up the Place de l'Eglise. This takes you back out into the open countryside, once again crossing the new spur of the N174.

> From St-Jean it is approximately 5km to the valley of the river Vire at Saint-Fromond. Follow its twisting course past the tiny commune of La Meauffe and on to the bridge at Pont-Hébert. Here you cross to the opposite bank and continue some 15km to Saint-Lô. It is a beautiful ride along the riverbank and just before St-Lô – to be precise, just before the sewage works – is a striking escarpment at the top of which is Agneaux, which faces Saint-Lô across the banks of the Vire. There is a rather splendid medieval chateau here which is now a hotel and restaurant. Otherwise, there are several hotels in the centre of Saint-Lô.

 **Where to sleep?**

Elevage des Ruettes, 50620 Saint Fromond.**02 33 56 82 84.**
www.lesRuettes.fr. lenoury.jean-louis@neuf.fr

 **Bike Shops**

Accro Vélo
200 avenue de Paris.
50000 Saint-Lô
02 33 75 67 30. accrovelo.fr

SAINT-LÔ

Saint-Lô has seen some action in its long and turbulent history, but none so devastating as the Battle of Normandy. In June 1940 the Germans muscled into town because its strategic importance in Lower Normandy, at the crossroads to Cherbourg, made it a vital stronghold.

It was therefore equally important for the Allies to get them out. In June 1944 American bombers began this process with a campaign that was to turn the course of the war. When Saint-Lô was liberated on the morning of July 19th the playwright Samuel Beckett was moved to nickname it 'la Capitale des Ruines'.

All but 5% of this handsome city, whose walls had been built by the Emperor Charlemagne 1200 years before, was still standing. Not much more than the Gothic spires of Notre-Dame church remained, along with a few houses in the suburbs, plus some of the walls and two towers of the old citadel.

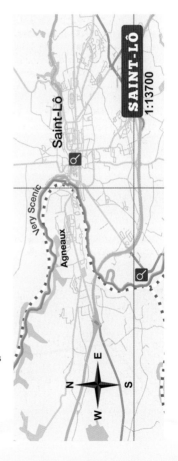

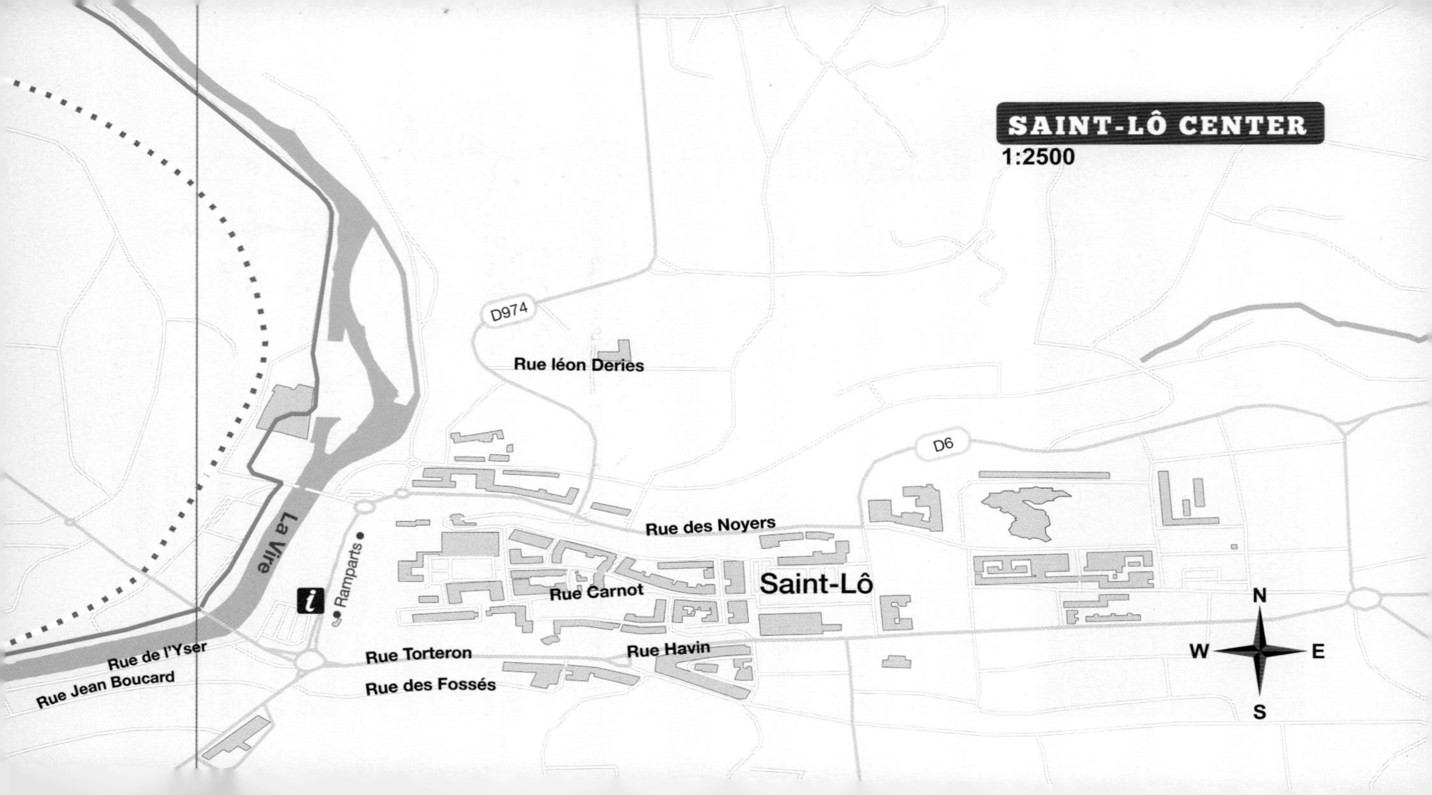

SAINT-LÔ CENTER

1:2500

N E S W

D6

D974

Rue léon Deries

Rue des Noyers

Saint-Lô

Rue Carnot

Rue Havin

Rue Torteron

Rue des Fossés

Ramparts

La Vire

Rue de l'Yser

Rue Jean Boucard

History in a nutshell

A quick note on previous horrors: Saint-Lô was twice 'part' of England: it was sacked by English troops during the Hundred Years War and was occupied between 1347 and 1378, and then again from 1418 to 1449.

The Vikings had also stormed in. So did the Protestant Huguenots, who took the town during the Wars of Religion in 1562, leading to its partial destruction by royal troops 12 years later. Continued persecution of the Protestants led to the town losing all its craftsmen, a grievous loss as its fame and fortune had been built on the back of its guild of tailors. But by the end of the 18th century it had bounced back and become capital of the Manche department and in 1858 a rail link to Paris was installed.

So 1944 was hardly the first time in its history that the townsfolk had had to pull themselves up by their own bootstraps. Saint-Lô is a vibrant place once again, though very far from elegant, as both fiscal and architectural poverty abounded when it was reconstructed.

 # Where to eat?

Le Péché Mignon, 84 Rue Maréchal Juin, 50000 Saint-Lô. Good value traditional cooking. **le-peche-mignon.monsite.orange.fr**

La Tour Carrée, Avenue Ste-Marie, 50180 Agneaux. About 2km from town, this is the gourmet restaurant attached to the Château d'Agneaux, in the 500 year old outbuilding. Great setting, good service and good food.

La Table de Louis, Avenue Ste-Marie, 50180 Agneaux. About 2km from town. It's the less expensive dining option at the Château d'Agneaux.

La Crémaillère, 10 Rue de la Chancellerie, 50000 Saint-Lô. **la-cremaillere-50.com**. **02 33 57 14 68**. Up on the ramparts. Menus from €9.50 (lunch time set meal).

Le Toucan, 24 Rue de Neufbourg, 50000 Saint-Lô. **02 33 57 09 01**. Breton Crêperie in the heart of Normandy.

Le Goût Sauvage, 10, Rue de Villedieu, 50000 Saint-Lo. **02 33 72 24 76. legoutsauvage.typepad.com**.

Where to sleep?

⑤⑤/⑤⑤⑤ Château d'Agneaux***, Avenue Sainte-Marie, Agneaux. **02 33 57 65 88**. **chateau-agneaux.com**. Charming medieval building. Good restaurant.

⑤⑤ Mercure***, Avenue Briovère, Saint-Lô. **02 33 05 10 84**. mercure. com. Town centre. **mercure.com**

⑤⑤ Best Hôtel**, 3 Parc Europe, Boulevard de Strasbourg, 50000 Saint-Lô. **02 33 57 57 57**. **besthotel.fr/Saint_lo.**

⑤⑤ Brit Hôtel, 130 Rue de la Liberté, 50000 Saint-Lô. **02 33 56 56 56**. **hotel-saint-lo.brithotel.fr**. Good value, good reviews.

⑤ Ibis, 594 Rue Jules Vallès, Saint-Lô. **02 33 57 78 38**. Bar and restaurant. 3km from town.

⑤ F1 Rue Jules Valles, PA la Chevalerie, 50000 Saint-Lô. **0891 70 53 84**.

♡ **⑤** La Crémaillère, 10 Rue de la Chancellerie, 50000 Saint-Lô. **la-cremaillere-50.com**. **02 33 57 14 68**. Up on the ramparts. Good value and well run. Restaurant and bar as well.

✱ THE BOCAGE

The region around Saint-Lô is known as the '*pays du Bocage*'. It is the sort of landscape often found in Devon. The word describes a terrain of mixed woodland and pasture, with fields and winding country lanes sunk between narrow ridges and banks topped by tall thick hedgerows. These act as wind breaks, but also limit visibility. During the Battle of Normandy they prevented tanks from advancing, so progress against the entrenched Germans had to be hand-to-hand, making for bloody combat. American personnel usually referred to bocage as 'hedgerows'. So very different from the flat landscape of East Anglia, where preparations for D-Day had taken place!

Apple and pear trees grow on the farms in the Vire bocage, so cider presses as well as dairies dot the landscape. The river itself has gouged a circuitous path through the rocky landscape, and the towpath faithfully follows it, right past Pont Farcy.

SAINT-LÔ TO PONT-FARCY

32km (20miles)

Challenge: Moderate

Route Info

▶ The cycle path now follows the valley of the Vire all the way to Condé-sur-Vire. To the left, the river, to the right the rail track. This is flat and easy-going. You will do the 12km to Condé quickly, but try and take your time and enjoy the rolling pastures and hedgerows, the wild flowers and picture postcard scenery. The towpath offers some outstanding views of the gorges and hills.

Worth Noting: the area is renowned not just for its crêpes, but also its beef, cheeses and offal (a must: 'andouille' – a delightful tripe sausage far nicer than it sounds - see page 92). Charcuterie is also rightly praised.

▶ Following the finest section of the Vire Valley through the Roches de Ham (Ham Rocks) the PTM passes villages and hamlets to the mediaeval town of Tessy-sur-Vire. The most striking bit is Ham Rocks, which veer 100m up from the path. If you have time it is worth a short detour along lanes rich in blackberries and hazelnuts and surrounded by apple orchards, to take in the view from the top.

> **Torigni-sur-Vire:** a handsome rural town 5km due east of the route whose centre is dominated by the 16th century Château de Matignon. This fine building owes much to Jacques de Matignon, who pumped vast resources into making it one of the most magnificent châteaux in the Manche area. In 1731 he became, through marriage to Louise Grimaldi, the Sovereign Prince of Monaco. Despite being flattened on June 12 1944 by American bombs, Matignon was completely restored.

 ## Accommodation nearby:

Hôtel de la Gare, Rue de la Gare, 50160 Saint-Amand. **02 33 56 13 32.**

Hôtel du Bocage, Les Landes, 50160, Gléville. **02 33 56 06 01.**

Campsite: Le Lac des Charmilles. **02 33 56 91 74.**
camping-lacdescharmilles.com.

Camping Municipal. Route de Tessy, 14380, Pont-Farcy
02 31 68 32 06. mairiedepontfarcy@orange.fr

Hard by Ham Rocks is the village of La Chapelle-sur-Vire, a favoured stopover amongst pilgrims en route for Mont-Saint-Michel since the 12th century. The church is neo-Gothic and contains two statues from the 14th and 16th centuries. The main altar, in white stone, boasts some fine alabaster reliefs from the 15th century and there is a permanent exhibition to the increasingly popular sport of pilgrimage.

There's also a huge picnic area near the towpath at the Way of the Cross.

PONT-FARCY

A quiet, charming village that has seen busier days. In the recent past it was a thriving commercial centre whose port – 100km from the coast – was used to ferry local produce to the wider world. Pont-Farcy is perched on a rocky outcrop and lies at the end of a series of gorges. There has been a crossing point on the Vire since Roman times, as Pont-Farcy marks a strategic point on the crossroads between Caen and Avranches, and Saint-Lô and Vire.

Farmhands and local workers gather at lunch time at the Hôtel Le Coq Hardi where the 'menu ouvrier' (workers special) at €11 offers splendid value. If you have worked up a thirst, you can work it off here: unlimited wine and cider are included in the price. It's a robust menu in a delightfully old fashioned setting. The bar and its open hearth have seen little change in the past century. Sadly no longer lets rooms.

'By the 12th century Pont-Farcy also provided shelter to untold thousands of pilgrims from all over Europe who spent successive nights at Caen, Villers-Bocage, Pont-Farcy and Villedieu-les-Poêles before first setting eyes on the sacred Mont-Saint-Michel,' says Christopher Long in his fascinating history of Pont-Farcy (**christopherlong. co.uk/pont-farcy**).

CALVADOS 75.8km (47.39miles)

 PONT-FARCY
TO MORTAIN

Pont-Farcy > La Ferrière-Harang = 15km (9.4miles)

La Ferrière-Harang > Vire = 18.4km (11.5miles)

Vire > Sourdeval = 24.2km (15.1miles)

Sourdeval > Mortain= 18.2km (11.4miles)

Challenge:

Medium. Some climbing at the beginning and a long but gentle climb out of Vire to Sourdeval. Some of the best scenery in Normandy. Roads and Greenway.

Route Info

 The route now follows quiet lanes, continuing on the other side of the D675, along La Mainterie parallel with the north bank of the Vire. After 4km head right onto the D306 and keep going, through the hamlets of Bure-les-Monts, Malloués and Campeaux, where you cross the D674. Don't rush here as you need to head 10m left before turning right for 40m and heading left up Le Bourg, which skirts the village centre. This becomes the D185.

NB The small but agreeable village of Campeaux has a tiny supermarket next door to Le Symbolic bar/brasserie where you can grab a snack. There is also a butcher's shop. Be careful of the busy main road.

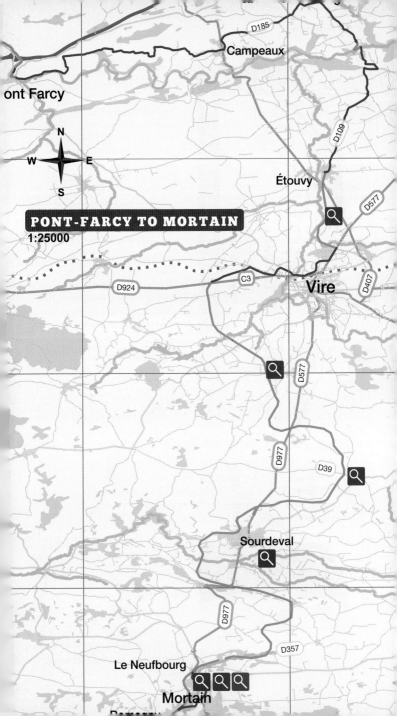

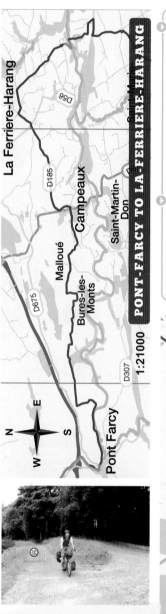

PONT-FARCY TO LA-FERRIÈRE-HARANG

1:21000

▷ After 4km you cross the D56 you are about 1km from La-Ferrière-Harang, a community of some 300 souls whose main claim to fame is its proximity to the bungee jumping venue at the Souleuvre Viaduct. The signs will take you just south of the village centre before heading south to the viaduct via the D185C.

▷ About 2km south of La Ferrière the route doglegs slightly before unexpectedly quitting the road in favour of a delightful stretch of Greenway, which will afford you great views of the viaduct.

SOULEUVRE VIADUCT

1:1300

✳ SOULEUVRE VIADUCT

It was built by Gustave 'The Tower' Eiffel, and its five towering arches span the valley of the Souleuvre river and were hewn from local granite for the Caen to Saint-Lô and Vire rail line. Opened in 1893 the viaduct was 365m long and 62.5m high at its highest point, and this is where a Mr A.J. Hackett set up his eponymous bungee operation in 1990. The bridge was a lifeline for the German encampment further north and, despite the best efforts of Allied bombers, it stood firm. In the summer of 1944 some 500 bombs were dropped on it. The line closed in 1960 and a decade later the station and lines were dynamited, leaving only Eiffel's five granite towers.

Bungee jumping: open daily in July and August. **02 31 66 31 66. ajhackett.fr**. At €89 you might find the price more breathtaking than the plunge.

LE-TROIS-CROIX

1:1300

Route de la Guérnière

D56

Le-Trois-Croix

N
W E
S

La Moissonnerie

○ Once you have followed the path through the woods you take a sharp right onto a minor road/track which takes you past the bungee jumping arch and the climb out of the valley and through Le Trois Croix, where you turn right onto the D56 and then left after 600m onto the D294A.

○ In 1.5km you will skirt the tiny Calvados community of Carville.

○ In a further 5km you will come to La Graverie where the Greenway veers off to the left as you go from the Rue de Bény Bocage into the Rue Etouvy. Keep your eyes open!

LA GRAVERIE

The village's most prominent feature (by far) is its high-spired church. 200m from the route is the Bar de la Poste which is also a newsagent and tobacconist (and boasts a pool table). Next door is a Viveco supermarket where you can stock up on most things if you are thinking of camping nearby. There is also a charcuterie selling cold meats and meals you can simply heat up. The chemist's shop (there's one in nearly every French settlement) is just round the corner.

Hôtel de la Gare, Place de la Gare: **02 31 68 20 16**. There's a huge dining room and bar with table football. Basic hotel with food, beer and beds.

○ This delightful section of *voie verte* will take you to the nearby outskirts of Vire, where you turn right onto the Rue de Caen, and so into the centre of Vire.

○ If you are not stopping here, then the route signs will take you right onto the Rue de Raymond Berthout, just before the big sports ground. This will skirt the centre and have you on your way to the old rail line that grinds its way up to Sourdeval.

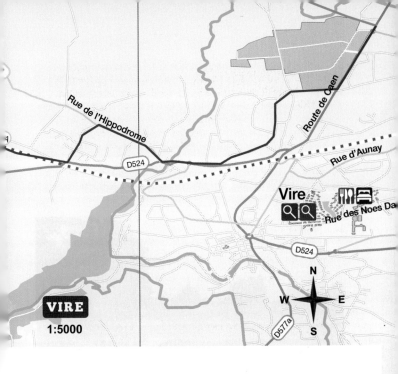

VIRE

Like St-Lô, Vire was a strategic cross roads for the occupying army and was duly bombed to virtual obliteration during the Battle of Normandy. You still get tantalising glimpses of how magnificent it must have been: the clock tower rises majestically above the main medieval town gate, flanked by sturdy fortified towers erected around the 14th century.

Vire was originally built on a small hill overlooking the bocage during the 8th century, before expanding hugely under the control of Henry I of England, a son of William the Conqueror. It became an important bastion for the Dukes of Normandy and remained a powerful stronghold until the Wars of Religion, when its strong protestant ties led to a political decline. In 1630 the castle was dismantled by France's most powerful politician, Cardinal Richelieu.

June 1944 saw the destruction of 95% of Vire and the subsequent reconstruction was only able to restore fragments of this once fine medieval fastness. A memorial to victims of the bombardment, next to the South Tower, was unveiled in 1960.

Vire is renowned for gastronomy, though its pride and joy might not to be everyone's taste: the andouille is a spicy sausage made from pig's intestines and is truly delicious so long as you are not faint-hearted. Another popular local dish is tripes a la mode, again an intestinal delight that fuelled the local paysans and workers at the cloth mills down in the valleys of the Varenne and Vire. The latter were fabled for their topical satirical drinking songs during the 15th century, known as 'vaux de Vire'. The fashion subsequently took off throughout Europe, acquiring the name 'vaux de Vire' and by around 1500 this had changed to 'voix de ville', before becoming part of the modern cultural landscape as the word 'vaudeville'.

 Points of interest

Office de Tourisme – Square de la Résistance. **02 31 66 28 50. bocage-normand.com.**

Eglise Notre-Dame, Place Notre-Dame. Gothic church dating from the 13th century. Beautiful restoration following lightning strikes, the Revolution and wars.

Tour de l'Horloge – Place 6 Juin. This is the old gate to the town comprising a 15th century belfry and twin towers.

Museum – 2 Place Ste-Anne. **02 31 68 10 49. museedevire.blogspot.fr**. Exhibitions of bocage culture and local painters.

Where to eat?

Manoir de la Pommeraie – 2.5km by D524, 14500 Vire.
02 31 68 07 71. manoirdelapommeraie.com. Fine dining at reasonable prices, with menus of varying prices so fits most pockets. 18th century manor house in a park on the edge of town.

Au Vrai Normand, 14 Rue Arman Gasté. **02 31 67 90 99. auvrainormand.com**. Classic Normandy cuisine. Has a faithful following and benefits from young talent from the local catering college.

Le Triskell, 17 Rue André Halbout. **02 31 68 00 66**. Offers cheap but well executed French dishes plus pizzas. Highly rated locally, and friendly (lunch for €10 with wine etc). Portions are generous and the owner Pascal speaks good English.

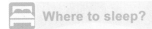

Where to sleep?

Hôtel St-Pierre**, 20 Avenue du Général Leclerc, Vire. **02 31 68 05 82. st-pierre-hotel-vire.fr**

Hôtel de France**, 4 Rue d'Aignaux, 14500 Vire. **02 31 68 00 35. hoteldefrancevire.com.**

Hôtel Moderne, 12 Place de la Gare, 14500 Vire. **02 31 68 01 39. hotel-moderne-vire.fr.**

Camponile Vire***, La Papillonnière, Route de Caen, 14500 Vire. **02 31 67 01 58. campanile.com/Hotels-Vire.**

Hôtel Restaurant Rêvotel, Avenue de Bischwiller, 14500 Vire. **02 31 66 18 66. revotel-vire.fr.**

Bike Hire & Repair

Cycles Du Bocage
30 route de Condé,14500 Vaudry
02 31 67 99 04. cyclesdubocage@orange.fr

 Where to drink?

Café du Commerce, 16 Rue du Général Leclerc. Typical French bar, doubling as a restaurant.

Le Gambrinus, 2 Rue Turpin. All purpose café, bar, restaurant. Specialises in beers.

Le Relais Fleuri, Rue Saint-Clair. Restaurant and pub in the town centre.

VIRE TO SOURDEVAL

24.2km (15.1miles)

 Challenge:

Moderate with some long but slow climbing. Greenway all the way.

Route Info

▶ Follow the Avenue Georges Pompidou and head right down the Avenue Guy de Maupassant taking the first exit from the roundabout along the Rue de Granville for 100m before it merges with the Rue de l'Hippodrome. Continue for about 800m then go left onto the Avenue de Franceville. After about 500m go right, onto the D185A which you follow for 1km before doglegging round Le Roussel farm. You are back on the Greenway in 1.5km, once past the railway crossing.

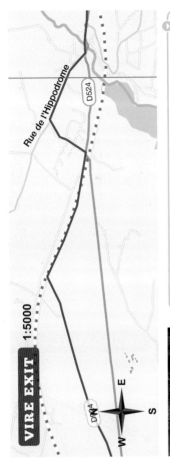

The section to Sourdeval involves some long but gentle climbing up the old railway line. With the exception of two short(ish) stretches of downhill there is an unremitting section of uphill (about 20km) once you're on the Greenway, but the countryside is delightful and the climbs are gentle (this is an old railway line). Calvados is rich in woodlands and wildlife, with rolling pastures, hillsides and steep valleys. It is Greenway all the way to Sourdeval and the highest point of climb is the old station at Les Maures, at 314m (1034ft) above sea level.

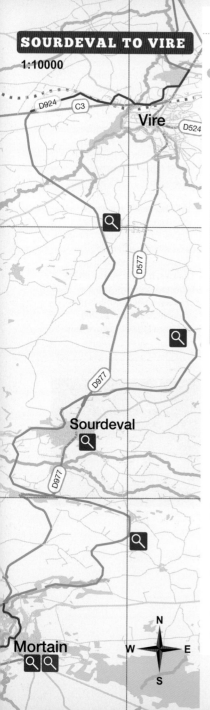

SOURDEVAL TO VIRE

1:10000

D924 C3

Vire

D524

D577

D977

Sourdeval

D977

Mortain

N
W — E
S

NB there is one section where you are very likely indeed to get lost (until better signage is erected). The Greenway runs alongside the D977 just before Sourdeval and a pedestrian tunnel goes under the road. Turn right at the end of the tunnel and head back up the hill. Keep your eyes open for PTM signs about 400m up the path. This section is counterintuitive as (a) you are heading back in the direction from which you have come and (b) there are no signs to tell you this is what you should be doing! You pick up the Greenway again on the left and this swings you into the pleasant and bustling village of Sourdeval.

SOURDEVAL DETAIL

1:600

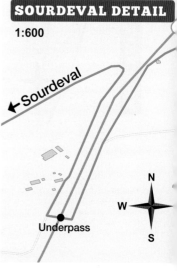

← Sourdeval

Underpass

N
W — E
S

History

This section of voie verte, which connects Vire with Mont-Saint-Michel, was built by Fulgence Bienvenüe, the Isambard Kingdom Brunel of French engineering. Bienvenüe was from just over the Brittany border and is more famed for building the Paris Métro, of which he was chief engineer for more than 30 years until retiring at 80 in 1932. This line was driven through 100km of hitherto impenetrable bocage and gave this landlocked and isolated corner of Normandy the economic lifeline it so desperately needed. The last passengers travelled the line just before the outbreak of war in 1939. Shortly afterwards the last goods train whistled a farewell to locomotion, and it was not until 1991 that the Manche tourist board had the great idea of restoring the line as a voie verte.

1911 witnessed a tragedy between Les Maures and St-Germain-de-Tallevende, when a train full of trippers hit a goods wagon on a blind bend at a combined speed of 90kmh. The goods wagon disintegrated and somehow landed on top of the passenger train, which was just short of the highest point, stopping it in its tracks. The brakes on the carriages were not working and the hapless tripper train started trundling backwards down the slope it had just climbed, towards Vire. A rail worker threw all the doors open and persuaded folk to jump before the train had reached a critical speed. Seven brave rail workers were killed, but all the passengers survived, with cuts and bruises. The train eventually came to a halt 6km away near St-Martin-de-Tallevende. Think of this as you bomb up the hill towards Les Maures!

SOURDEVAL

There's a big main square and a helpful tourist office in the Place Charles de Gaulle (**02 33 79 35 61. sourdevaltourisme.fr**). Next to the church are some handy public conveniences.

Sourdeval has plenty of B&Bs and small hotels, a couple of restaurants and shops so makes it an ideal place to consider stopping over.

Where to eat?

Restaurant Le Commerce, 21 Rue du Général Millet, 50150 Sourdeval. **02 33 59 97 04.**

Crêperie Beurre et Confiture, 24 Place Charles de Gaulle, 50150 Sourdeval. **09 81 35 30 03.**

Café de Pays Le Bô'Bar, 15 Rue Saint Martin, 50150 Sourdeval. **02 33 69 33 66.**

Auberge du Moulin, 4 le Moulin, 50150 Brouains. **02 33 59 50 60.** About 7km west of Sourdeval. Also does accommodation (see below). High quality cooking.

Hôtel des Voyageurs, 7 Place du Champ de Foire, 50150 Sourdeval. **02 33 59 61 50**. Good value French staples.

Le Relais des Routiers, 1 Place du Champ de Foir, 50150 Sourdeval. **02 33 59 62 91.** Cheap for lunch. Solid provincial fare.

 Where to sleep?

♥ ⓔⓔ **Manoir de Clérisson**, 50150 Sourdeval. **02 33 59 64 57 or 06 98 90 03 94. manoirdeclerisson.e-monsite. com**. Francoise Foscher. Superb B&B. 1 guest room and a loft conversion ideal for a group of 3. Massage and shiatsu on offer. Very cycle friendly. Possibly the finest breakfast spread this author has encountered!

ⓔ **Auberge du Moulin**, 4 le Moulin, 50150 Brouains. **02 33 59 50 60. aubergedumoulin.net.** About 7km west of Sourdeval, a lovely setting with a good restaurant. 2 rooms.

ⓔ **Hôtel des Voyageurs**, 7 Place du Champ de Foire, 50150 Sourdeval. **02 33 59 61 50**. Basic 6 room hotel with a restaurant.

ⓔ **Le Relais des Routiers**, 1 Place du Champ de Foire, 50150 Sourdeval. **02 33 59 62 91**. Basic 5 room hotel with a restaurant.

CAMPSITES

Le Potager, Chemin du Potager, 50150 Sourdeval. Open 1 May to 30 Sept. 11 pitches. €4.50 for first person, €2.50pp thereafter. Lock-up and hook-ups. Near town centre. **02 33 79 35 55 or 02 33 79 35 61.**

Camper van park, Rue Jean-Baptiste Janin, 50150 Sourdeval. **02 33 79 35 55**. Free electricity and water, plus sanitary refuse dump.

GROUP ACCOMMODATION

La Pelleterie, 50150 Sourdeval. **02 33 59 66 23 or 06 73 75 88 15**. **pagesperso-orange.fr/gite-see-rousse**. Sleeps 13. €17 per night.

SOURDEVAL TO MORTAIN

18km (11.3m)

Challenge: Easy. Greenway all the way.

Route Info

- Sourdeval to Mortain is only 18km, but it's worth taking your time as you travel through more stunning woodlands and valleys with rivers and waterfalls. The Cance, Sée and Cancon weave their watery courses port, starboard and amidships as the tree-lined Vire to Mortain rail line makes its majestic crossing of the bocage before pitching up at Mortain. This is one of the lovelier stages of the ride.

- At Mortain the River Cance tumbles through rocky gorges down to the wooded basin of the Sélune river, creating the two spectacular sets of waterfalls. La Grande Cascade and La Petite Cascade are must-sees. The latter is the biggest in the north west corner of France and the backdrop is perfect for a leisurely picnic lunch or stopover in Mortain.

- The track is excellent – compacted sand and gravel, easy going for any bike except perhaps after prolonged downpours when it can get a tad muddy and become harder work.

LOWER NORMANDY 65km (40.6miles)

LE BOCAGE MORTAINAIS –

 MORTAIN TO
MONT-SAINT-MICHEL

Mortain > St-Hilaire-du-Harcouët = 14.9km (9.3miles)
St-Hilaire-du-Harcouët > Ducey = 19km (11.9miles)
Ducey > Mont-Saint-Michel = 31.1km (19.4miles)

 Challenge:

Easy. Lanes to start then Greenway to Pontaubault, then quiet lanes to Mont-Saint-Michel

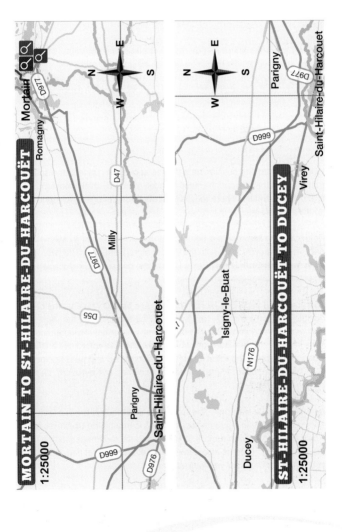

MORTAIN TO ST-HILAIRE-DU-HARCOUËT

1:25000

Mortain
Romagny
D977
D47
Milly
D977
D55
Parigny
D999
D976
Sain-Hilaire-du-Harcouet

N E S W

ST-HILAIRE-DU-HARCOUËT TO DUCEY

1:25000

Parigny
D977
D999
Virey
Saint-Hilaire-du-Harcouet
Isigny-le-Buat
N176
Ducey

N E S W

MORTAIN

 ## History in a nutshell

Mortain was the fulcrum of the Battle of Normandy in August 1944. The counter-attack by the Germans was designed to isolate the American positions further west in Brittany, but it back-fired and after a bloody six-day battle the Wehrmacht and SS Panzer divisions suffered severe losses and were forced to withdraw. Thus did Mortain become yet another ruined city on the war-scarred map of Normandy.

However its striking position on a hillside above the plains to the south make it an attractive and dramatic location, offset by thick woodlands and great waterfalls where the Cance cuts through Basse-Normandie's southernmost hills.

Below lies the basin of the Sélune, the river which winds its way – parallel to the cycle route – to the Bay of Mont-St-Michel. The twin waterfalls, the Grande and Petite Cascades, carve their way through the limestone to disgorge into the Sélune.

The voie verte bypasses Mortain but it would be a crying shame not to deviate and come through Neufbourg via the route de la Gare, past the imposing 12th century Abbaye Blanche, now a nunnery. You cannot miss its more modern addition, which looks like a Bradford mill and lies close to the road. The route into town is signposted and passes close to the Grande Cascade. There is a handy bike shop at Neufbourg, plus a couple of restaurants.

In addition to the waterfalls, the Collégiale St-Evroult is worth a look: a 13th century Gothic church whose treasury contains the Chrismal, an Anglo-Irish casket with runic inscriptions and sacred images dating from the 7th century. There is also a lively market and several places to stock your panniers or take a well-earned break.

Office de Tourisme, Rue du Bourglopin. **02 33 59 19 74. ville-mortain.fr.**

Le Neufbourg

Blanche Abbey

Grande Cascade
(Waterfall)

Petit Cascade

River Cance

Rue du Rocher

Rue de la 30ème Division

Mortain

Rue du Rocher

Parking

D977

D205

D977

MORTAIN VIA NEUFBOURG

1:2500

Where to eat & drink?

Hôtel de la Poste, 1 Place des Arcades, 50140 Mortain.

Hôtel au Bon Vent, 64 Rue du Rocher, 50140 Mortain.

Hôtel les Closeaux Phil, Route de Saint-Hilaire-du-Harcouët, 50140 Romagny. You pass Romagny en route out of Mortain.

 Where to sleep?

CENTRE OF MORTAIN

♡ 💷💷/💷💷💷 Hôtel de la Poste, 1 Place des Arcades. **02 33 59 00 05. hoteldelaposte.fr.** Proud looking town centre place with 27 rooms. Under new ownership. Rooms from €55.

💷 Hôtel Au Bon Vent, 64 Rue du Rocher. **02 33 59 00 68**. 5 rooms. Non-classified.

B&B
Derek & Sue Powell, 43 bis Rue du Rocher, 50140 Mortain. **02 33 50 06 39**. 2 rooms, €50 a room.

CAMPING
♡ Camping les Cascades, Place du Château, 50140 Mortain. **02 33 79 30 30. ville-mortain.fr**. Open from Easter until 30 Sept. 16 pitches. Also space for camper vans.

BUNKHOUSE
Gîte de Groupes La Cance, Mairie de Neufbourg, Rue du Croissant, 50140 Le Neufbourg, Mortain. **02 33 59 18 55 or 06 71 25 26 25. le-neufbourg.fr.st**. €11 to €12 a night. Dormitories for 2/5/6 people sleeping 21 in total. Lock up for bikes and sheet hire.

MORTAIN TO DUCEY

Challenge: Easy. Nearly all Greenway.

Route Info

▶ If you are leaving from the centre of Mortain head down the Rue du Bassin going left into the place du Château and Rue du Moulin Foulier (D133) until it links up with the voie verte. There are a couple of doglegs so look out for signs. At the junction with the D601 head right, following the voie verte.

▶ You will soon pass Romagny.

💷Hôtel les Closeaux Phil, Route de Saint-Hilaire-du-Harcouët, 50140 Romagny. **02 33 61 41 45 or 06 37 34 51 76**. Just beyond Mortain but close to the route. 8 rooms. Lock up for bikes, free wi-fi. Sauna.

▶ Mortain marks the crossroads for the Petit Tour de Manche and another route, la Véloscénie. The voie verte now follows the old steam-train tracks which lead out to St-Hilaire-du-Harcouët, Ducey and on to the Bay of Mont-Saint-Michel, parallel with the serpentine course of the river Sélune. The countryside here is called the bocage Mortainais and runs dreamily through the pastoral plains towards the sea.

▶ It is easy cycling from here. St-Hilaire-du-Harcouët is 15km, with Ducey a further 19km.

ST-HILAIRE-DU-HARCOUËT

Originally a Viking settlement, St-Hilaire is now a vibrant market town (Wednesdays), with a famous livestock market. It boasts a public swimming lake, a public swimming pool with sauna and a Centre d'Art Sacré. There are also a few restaurants and hotels.

St-Hilaire was for centuries a military stronghold between the oft-quarreling regions of Normandy, Brittany and, to the south, the pays de la Loire. But since the 15th century commerce has been its mainstay. The town is dominated by the market square, the crossroads and the fine twin-towered church.

Office de Tourisme, Place du Bassin. **02 33 79 38 88.**
st-hilaire.fr/office_de_tourisme.htm.

Where to sleep?

£ £ **Le Cygne et Résidence*****, 99 Rue Waldeck Rousseau on the Fougères road. **02 33 49 11 84. hotellecygne.com**. 30 rooms. Splendid stop-off with a terrace.

£ **L'Agriculture**, 79-81 Rue Waldeck Rousseau. **02 33 49 10 60. hoteldelagriculture.com**. Comfortable, unpretentious and cheap. 16 rooms.

Camping municipal La Sélune Rue de Marly. **02 33 49 43 74. www.st-hilaire.fr**

 ## Eat & drink?

Both of the above have good restaurants. Le Cygne has a good wine list and specializes in Normandy and seafood dishes.

> More Greenway, all the way to Ducey, weaving its way through the heart of the bocage Mortainais. You will have gathered by now that much of the southern half of Normandy is bocage - the wooded countryside characteristic of northern France, with small irregular-shaped fields and many hedges and copses (as previously described). There are subtle variations between each area, you will notice.

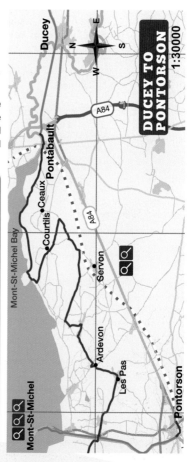

DUCEY

Henry V of England (and Agincourt) captured Ducey in 1418 during the Hundred Years War. This is a handsome little town dominated by the Château de Montgomery, an elegant house of the early 17th century, which sits on the banks of the Sélune. The river is the other main feature and there's a fine medieval bridge spanning it. The château was built by Gabriel II of Montgomery, whose father accidentally killed the French king, Henry II, in a jousting tournament held to celebrate the Peace of Cateau-Cambrésis at the conclusion of the Eighth Italian War. He himself perished on the scaffold during the Wars of Religion, for being a Protestant.

Ducey prides itself on being a ville fleurie, or floral town: each summer 25,000 flowers bloom in and around the centre. It has all the usual amenities of a small town and plenty to tempt you to spend a night here near the bay.

Office de Tourisme, 4 Rue du Génie. **02 33 60 21 53**.

 ## Where to eat & drink?

Auberge de la Sélune, 2 Rue Saint Germain. **02 33 60 25 25**. Gastronomic cuisine. €13 for lunch, dinner from €20.

La Marionnette, 2 Rue de Les Chéris. **02 33 58 84 29**. Traditional local fare plus pizzas, salads and grill. Menus €14.50 to €22.

Les Sens de Ciel, 44 Rue du Génie. **02 33 58 66 96**. Just does lunch. Popular with locals and closed weekends. €11 set meal ('menu ouvrier').

Le Ty Breizh, 27, Grande Rue. **02 33 48 47 48**. Crêperie. €9.80 to €17.50.

L'Oasis, 56, Grande Rue. Café, ideal for snacks or picnic lunch

Beer bar
Bar des Sportifs, 9 Place du Général de Gaulle. **02 33 48 46 73**. Has its own brewery. Does sandwiches, but bigger on beer than food.

 **Where to sleep?**

€€/€€€ **Moulin de Ducey*****, 1 Grand Rue. **02 33 60 25 25. moulindeducey.com**. This is a Best Western mill conversion on the banks of the Sélune. Buffet breakfast €11. 28 rooms.

€€ **Auberge de la Sélune****, 2 Rue Saint Germain. **02 33 48 53 62. selune.com.** Comfortable, 20 rooms, bar and restaurant. Free wifi.

CAMPSITE

Camping Municipale de Ducey, Rue de Boishue. **02 33 48 46 49 or 02 33 60 21 53. ducey-tourisme.com.** 33 pitches. Price per person: €2.90. Children under-7 €1.60. Pitch €1.40. Vehicle: €0.80. Electricity: €1.90.

B&B

107, Bois Herbert, 50220 Poilley. **02 33 58 60 04 or 06 98 92 38 11. legrillon2@wanadoo.fr**. Just outside Ducey. 1 room which can sleep up to 4. €40 for single occupancy, €70 for a group of 4.

Les Sources, 5 Lentille, 50220 Poilley. **02 33 68 21 89. gites-les-sources**.com. 4 rooms. Groups up to 10. From €21.25 to €60.

Caquerel, 50220 50220 Poilley. **02 33 48 52 45 or 06 72 11 22 51**. 3 rooms sleeping up to 7. From €16 to €35.

La Châtière, 8, Rue Patton, 50220 Pontaubault. **02 33 60 48 22. gouinlachatiere@wanadoo.fr**. 3 rooms sleeping up to 6. From €15 to €25.

DUCEY TO
MONT-SAINT-MICHEL

31.1km (19.4miles)

Challenge: Easy. Greenway to Pontaubault then lanes.

Route Info

▷ The Greenway takes you straight to the outskirts of Pontaubault where it comes to an end at the bailey bridge across the Sélune. Here you turn left along a lane and you are shortly in Pontaubault. A spur off the route goes up to Avranches, on the other side of the bay. This is for those wishing to meander a little further afield and does not reconnect with your route, so you have to retrace your steps.

▷ Go right at the T-junction, more or less opposite Chez Arsène, a roadside restaurant and bar. In 100m you will turn left onto the Rue de la Grève (D113), which follows the Sélune to the Baie de Mont-St-Michel, near Courtils. This is a magnificent stretch of the ride, along polders (dikes) with sweeping views of the panoramic bay.

PONTAUBAULT AND THE SURROUNDING AREA

You will have passed Pontaubault Bridge (but hopefully not gone over it). This is where General Patton's III Army crossed on August 1 1944 as part of Operation Cobra.

The stretch between Pontaubault and Mont-St-Michel is dotted with hotels and chambres d'hôtes as this is a major tourist destination, so you would be well advised to book your accommodation in advance.

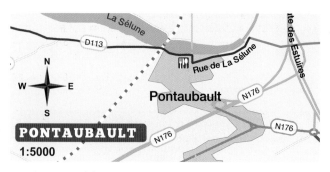

 **Where to sleep?**

In the Bay area. Many of these establishments have wonderful views.

HOTELS

£ Au Petit Quinquin**, 9 Les Forges, Route de Courtils, 50220 Céaux. **02 33 70 97 20. aupetitquinquin@wanadoo.fr www.aupetitquinquin.com**. 18 rooms.

£ Brit Hôtel-Restaurant**, La Buvette, 50220 Céaux. **02 33 70 92 55. relaisdumont@brithotel.fr www.hotel-mont-saint-michel.com**. 28 rooms

♡ **££/£££** Le Manoir de la Roche Torin***, 34, Route de la Roche Torin 50220 Courtils. **02 33 70 96 55. manoir.rochetorin@ wanadoo.fr www.manoir-rochetorin.com.** 15 rooms. Smart country house hotel with a view of Mont-St-Michel.

£ Hôtel-Bar-Restaurant**, D.275 Quartier de la Rive, 50170 Ardevon. **02 33 68 26 70. aubergedelabaie.fr**. 32 rooms.

B&B

La Goutte, 16 Rue de la Roche Thorin, 50220 Courtils. **02 33 48 59 34** or **06 09 07 36 15. annickhingan@hotmail.fr. www.gite-mont-saint-michel.net**. 3 rooms, sleeps up to 6. From €22 to €34.

La Guintré, 82 Route du Mont-Saint-Michel, 50220 Courtils. **02 33 60 06 02. www.gîtedefrance.com. lemoine.osack@club-internet.fr.** 5 rooms sleeping up to 11. From €16 to €30.

La Ruette, 2 Route de la Roche Torin, 50220 Courtils. **02 33 70 95 90 or 06 66 57 26 22. site.voila.fr/fermedelaRuette. lemouland.marie-pierre@ club-internet.fr.** 5 rooms, sleeps 15. From €16 to €42 (single occ).

L'Antre de Brocéliande, 6 Route des Vallées, 50220 Courtils. **02 14 13 42 61 or 06 30 51 12 45. martine.menager@neuf.fr. lantredebroceliande.com**. 3 rooms, sleeps 13. From €23 to €50.

BUNKHOUSE

Mme Elie Lemoine, 79, Route du Mont Saint-Michel. 50220 Courtils. **02 33 60 13 16**. 4 rooms, sleeps 18. Dormitory for 9. €10 per night.

CAMPING

35 Route du Mt-St-Michel, 50220 Courtils. **02 33 70 96 90. campingsaintmichel.com**. 75 pitches, 25 campervans. 3-star campsite with pool and lots of other facilities. From €10 to €21.

47 Route Saint Grégoire, 50170 Servon. **02 33 60 26 03. camping-mont-saint-michel.com**. 72 pitches. Swimming pool, pétanque (bowls), barbecue area. From €11.30 to €17.40.

Route Info

▶ Follow the dike-road (D113 then D313) past cultivated fields. The river and bay are never more than a few hundred metres to your right. You will soon skirt the attractive village of Céaux (off to your left) then Courtils and Huisnes-sur-Mer.

▶ Huisnes was liberated by American troops on 1 August 1944 and there is an ossuary where 11,956 German soldiers lie in 68 crypts dug into the hillside. The route now heads briefly inland through Ardevon, Les Pas, Beauvoir and La Grève.

▶ You will pass through the salt marshes where some of the finest tasting sheep are put out to graze. The salty grass informs the flavour of the meat (agneaux de pré salé) and produces a unique succulence. Worth looking out for on local menus!

▶ Here you can turn right to visit Mont-St-Michel, left to Pontorson (a good overnight destination) or simply cross the river Couesnon to continue towards Saint-Malo.

▶ There are hotels galore in this neighbourhood. We list only a selection of the best. If you are put off by vast numbers of trippers and don't fancy leaving your bike while you walk around Mont-St-Michel (bikes are not allowed into the citadel but there is an area at the foot where you can lock them to bike stands) then Pontorson is definitely a good bet. It is anything but touristy, offering decent and modestly priced rooms and some good and inexpensive eateries.

▶ If you stay at a hotel near the Mount, then you can of course, leave your bike locked up there and go on foot. It is a spectacular, iconic setting which bursts out of the sands like a volcano.

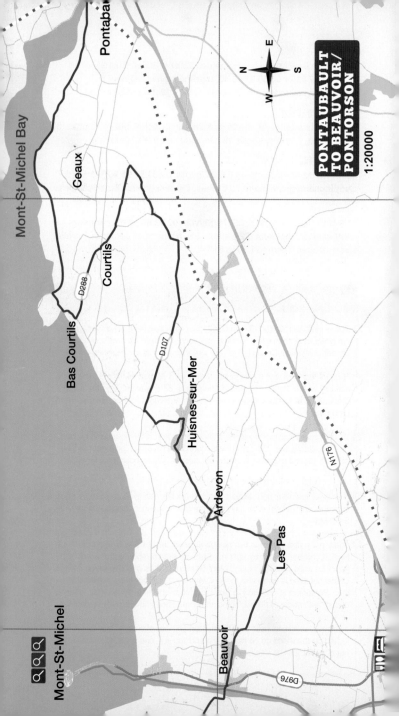

PONTAUBAULT
TO BEAUVOIR/
PONTORSON

1:20000

Mont-St-Michel Bay

Mont-St-Michel

Pontaba...

Ceaux

Courtils

Bas Courtils

D288

D107

Huisnes-sur-Mer

Ardevon

Les Pas

Beauvoir

D976

N176

PONTORSON

9km from Mont-Saint-Michel.

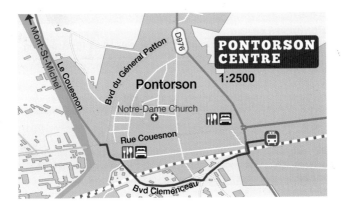

There are quite a few hotels here, plus a railway station. The latter has seen busier days, with only three or four trains stopping here daily. Pontorson was first settled by the Saxons then became a fortified town shortly after the death of William the Conqueror. Its high point probably came in the 14th century when Bertrand de Guesclin made it the capital for jousting and combat tournaments.

The church was founded by William the Conqueror as a mark of gratitude to the Virgin Mary, who apparently intervened to save his troops from drowning in the quicksands bordering the Couesnon. The scene is depicted in the Bayeux tapestry and in one of the stained glass windows of the 11th century edifice.

It is the last town in Normandy before Brittany, and there's a regular bus service to the Mount, so you could overnight here and still visit the World Heritage Site.

Office du Tourisme, Place de l'Hôtel-de-Ville. **02 33 60 20 65. mont-saint-michel-baie.com**.

Where to eat & drink?

Before Pontorson: Auberge du Terroir, 50170 Servon.
02 33 60 17 92. It's 10km before Pontorson in an old presbytery. Great value, generous portions and fine local cooking. There are also 6 rooms.

Pontorson centre
Hôtel de la Tour Brette, 8 Rue de Couesnon. **02 33 60 10 69**. Bustling and often full, this is an excellent and cheap spot for a wholesome, no-frills traditional French meal.

Le Grillon, 37 Rue de Couesnon. **02 33 60 17 80**. A splendid crêperie on the high street offering traditional dishes too. Rustic interior. Review highly favourable.

La Casa de Quentin, 102 Rue Saint-Michel. **02 33 33 48 61 95**. Great reviews, again. The pocket guide Petit Futé says you can eat crêpes and traditional dishes 'without abusing your wallet.'

Le Squadra, 102 Rue Couesnon. **02 33 68 31 17**. Helpful, cheerful and cheap. No airs and graces. Ideal for lunch.

Hôtel de Bretagne, 56 Rue de Couesnon. **02 33 60 10 55**. Classical French cooking, good wine list. Semi-formal and well executed. Good place for a leisurely supper.

Le Relais Gascon, 15 Rue de Tanis. **02 33 58 20 96**. le-relais-gascon.com. The chefs are from the Aveyron in the Midi-Pyrénées. Imaginative use of fish from the bay, tripe and other traditional French dishes. Also a bar.

Where to sleep?

 Hôtel de la Tour Brette**, 8 Rue de Couesnon. 02 33 60 10 69. Simple and comfortable. Free wifi. Helpful staff.

Hôtel Montgomery (Best Western)***, 13 Rue de Couesnon. 02 33 60 00 09. hotel-montgomery.com. Ivy clad and old fashioned. Most attractive building on the high street.

Hôtel Ariane***, 50 Bvd Clémenceau. 02 33 60 03 84. ariane-mt-st-michel.com. Ideal for large groups. Comfortable and modern, near station.

B&B
Les Belles de Mai, 35 Rue Saint-Michel. **02 33 58 47 79.**
Chambresdhotesmontsaintmichel.com.

▶ If you have skipped Pontorson, you turn right to visit the Mount or
go straight over the bridge to follow the route.

MONT-SAINT-MICHEL

We have the Archangel Michael
to thank for this miracle of
architecture rising out of the sea
and sand. He appeared in a dream
to Aubert, Bishop of Avranches,
back in the 8th century. Aubert
duly built an oratory atop the rocky
island. Then came the abbey,
followed by the other magnificent
granite buildings such as the
Gothic Chancel that clusters the
summit of the Mount, resembling
the hands of a supplicant in prayer.

As a feat of construction, it was
an achievement on a par with
anything in Europe: great slabs
of granite were hauled to the top
to construct the Romanesque
church. This meant building mighty
foundations into the rock-face.
The pattern of its construction
represented feudal society: at the
top was God, in the form of the
abbey and monastery; below this
the great halls; then stores and
housing, and at the bottom, outside
the walls, the humble abodes of
fishermen and farmers.

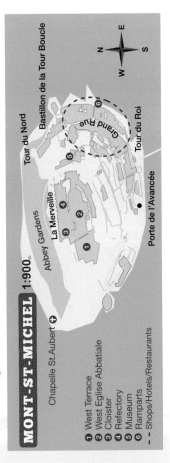

MONT-ST-MICHEL 1:900

❶ West Terrace
❷ West Eglise Abbatiale
❸ Cloister
❹ Refectory
❺ Museum
❻ Ramparts
- - Shops/Hotels/Restaurants

It occupies 247 acres, has 44 permanent residents (compared with 268 in 1954), is 92 metres high at its highest point and was so thoroughly fortified that it withstood a 30-year siege.

A tidal causeway used to connect Mont-Saint-Michel to the mainland. The track was covered at high tide and revealed at low tide. But in June 2006 a €250 million project to build a hydraulic dam was launched using tidal waters and the river Couesnon to help remove the accumulated silt (building up at a rate of 1,000,000 tons a year) deposited by the rising tides, and to make Mont Saint-Michel an island again. It became a UNESCO World Heritage site in 1979. For up to date information on the programme visit **projetmontstmichel.fr**.

The great French writer Victor Hugo described the tide as moving 'as swiftly as a galloping horse'. These treacherous tides can vary greatly by up to 15 metres between high and low water. Pilgrims dubbed it 'St. Michael in peril of the sea', and the mount can still pose dangers for visitors who avoid the causeway and attempt the hazardous walk across the sands.

Whether shrouded in mist or set like a jewel by the setting sun, Mont-Saint-Michel conjures up as much mystery and beauty now as it did in medieval times. Pilgrims (many in buses) pour onto the rock every day.

INFORMATION

Office de Tourisme 02 33 60 14 30. ot-montstmichel.com. 9 am – 7 pm
July & August. 9 am 12.30 pm & 2 pm – 6 pm other times of the year.

The Abbey: open daily except the 1st of January, the 1st of May and
the 25th of December. From 2 May to 31 August: 9 am to 7 pm, last
admission at 6 pm. From 1 September to 30 April: 9.30 am to 6 pm, last
admission at 5 pm.

BOOKING AND INFORMATION
02 33 89 80 00. mont-saint-michel.monuments-nationaux.fr.

Abbey Steps: 90 of them rise from the Abbot's buildings.

West Platform for panoramic views of the Bay.

La Merveille – the Marvel. This is the name given to the Gothic
buildings on the north side of the mount. These are the Refectory, the
Guests' Hall, Cloisters and the Almonry, all built in the early 13th century.

 ## Where to eat & drink?

The mount is dotted with crêperies and snack bars. Here are a few samples:

Caféteria La Belle Normande
 02 33 60 45 55. lemontsaintmichel.info
Self-service, snack, continuous service, take away.

Pancake bar brasserie Le Chapeau Rouge
02 33 60 14 29 / 06 71 18 23 94. le-chapeau-rouge-mont-st-michel.com
Menus: from 13 € to 19,90 € , groups bookings on request, 60 seats.

Restaurant Chez Mado
02 33 60 14 08.chezmado.fr
menus from €14 till €26, groups bookings on request, 300 seats.

Traditional pancake bar La Cloche (open from the beginning of
February till 30th of November 2013 and during Christmas holidays)
 02 33 60 15 65. choucas1999@live.fr
Homemade pancakes and buckwheat pancakes. Menus: 9,90 € and
15,50 € and carte, 42 seats. Pancake bar, bar, ice-cream, salads.
Recommended on Tripadvisor.

Bar Restaurant La Confiance
02 33 60 14 07. la-confiance.fr. Menus from €13 till €25. 100 seats.

Restaurant Le Saint-Michel
02 33 60 14 37. lesaintmichelridel.com
Menus €16. Restaurant and crêperie. 54 seats.

 ## Where to sleep?

HOTELS AT THE ENTRANCE OF THE CAUSEWAY
(2 kilometres before Mont Saint-Michel):

Hôtel Formule Verte** (open from the 16th of February till the 10th of November 2013) **02 33 60 14 13. le-mont-saint-michel.com**. 45 rooms from €50-€66 (2 pers). Menus from €11 plus a la carte, 500 seats.

Hôtel Saint Aubert** **02 33 60 08 74. saint-aubert.com**
27 rooms €85 - €130, groups bookings on request. Menus from €16 - €24.

Hôtel Vert** **02 33 60 09 33. le-mont-saint-michel.com**
54 rooms from €64,50 - €81,50 (2 pers). Menus from €11.

INSIDE THE WALLS

Hôtel du Guesclin** (open from the 30th of March till the 11th of November 2013) **02 33 60 14 10. hotelduguesclin.com**
10 rooms from €78 - €93. Menus from €19. Half board from €73.

Hôtel le Mouton Blanc**
02 33 60 14 08 lemoutonblanc.fr. 15 rooms from €115. Menus from €18.

Hôtel la Vieille Auberge **
02 33 60 14 34. lavieilleauberge-montsaintmichel.com
11 rooms from €120. Restaurant, menus and carte, brasserie and pancake bar.

Hôtel Saint Michel
02 33 60 02 16: www.hotel-saintmichel.com. 6 rooms from €75.

Logis Saint Sebastian. **02 33 60 14 08.**
logis-saint-sebastien.com 3 rooms from €55.

BRITTANY   62km (38.7miles)

MONT-ST-MICHEL TO SAINT-MALO

Mont-Saint-Michel > Le Vivier-sur-Mer = 29.2km (18.3miles)
Le Vivier-sur-Mer > Cancale = 17km (10.7miles)
Cancale> Saint-Malo = 15.6km (9.8miles)

Challenge:

Easy. Shared Greenway and roads all the way

This chapter takes you through some prime tourism country where some very fine dining is to be had. There is plenty to see, the route is easy to follow, so much of the following information will be devoted to winkling out those places where you might wish to while away some time and put back on some of those calories you will have lost in the last few days.

It also takes you through the best gastronomic area of the trip so more restaurant detail has been included here.

MONT-SAINT-MICHEL TO LE VIVIER-SUR-MER

29.2km (18.3miles)

Challenge:

Easy, though the shared Greenway between Roz-de-Couesnon can be tricky in heavy rain. Be wary on the seafront road as it can get very busy.

Route Info

▶ If coming from Pontorson join the river Couesnon near the end of Rue de Couesnon. There is a lovely pathway along the right bank of the river as you head towards the Mount. The marshland either side of the river is full of wildlife and the canalized river lined with trees, giving the impression of a watery driveway to the ancient citadel.

▶ You pass Moidrey on your right and either (a) continue past Beauvoir to visit the pilgrim magnet, or (b) hang a left and follow the wonderful polders (dikes). This left turn comes after around 7km. Welcome to Brittany!

If *not* going on to Mont-Saint-Michel, go right at the first crossroads for 1km then left, heading inland in the direction of Pontorson.

The landscape is flat and fertile and behind you looms Mont-Saint-Michel. Don't forget to stop and admire. Head right after 4km, onto

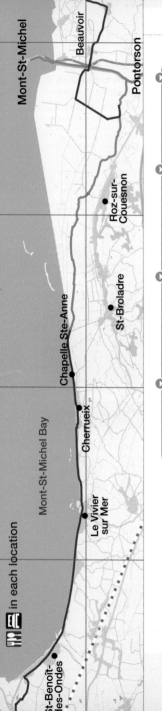

Mont-St-Michel

Beauvoir

Pontorson

Roz-sur-Couesnon

St-Broladre

Chapelle-Ste-Anne

Mont-St-Michel Bay

Cherrueix

Le Vivier sur Mer

St-Benoît-des-Ondes

in each location

- a magnificent raised Greenway that takes you past Roz-sur-Couesnon. The Greenway, shared with walkers and horse riders, stretches on for about 12km before you come to La Chapelle-Ste-Anne, on the sea front.

- **But be warned:** this stretch is far from ideal for a road bike. It is rutted and can be rough going in the wet. It is easy enough on a touring bike but those with skinny tyres and top of the range road bikes might wish to take the D797 instead.

- This is more of a voie brune than voie verte. The Greenway comes to an abrupt end after about 8km and there were no signs at time of going to press. Head left down the road and you will very shortly pick up a sign for where the Greenway continues to Chapelle-Ste-Anne.

- The next stretch takes you along the shoreline, through Cherrueix, Le Vivier-sur-Mer, Hirel, St-Benoît-des-Ondes, St-Méloir-des-Ondes and up to the outskirts of Cancale, one of Brittany's prettiest seaside resorts.

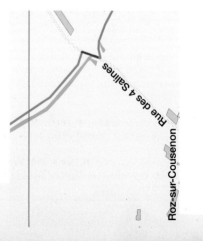

Rue des 4 Salines

Roz-sur-Cousenon

This whole area is packed with accommodation and restaurants and is fully geared up for tourism. If the area proves to be solidly booked up – not beyond the realms of possibility – then a 9km detour to Dol-de-Bretagne might be necessary

Office de Tourisme 02 99 48 15 37. pays-de-dol.com

Dol-de-Bretagne is a handsome town with a fine cathedral and much else to commend it. The cathedral of Saint-Samson has a nave as long as a football pitch and the town centre has some fine medieval architecture.

CHERRUEIX

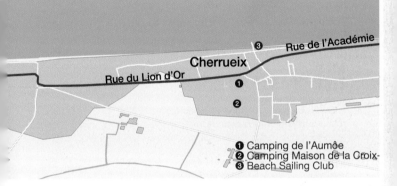

❶ Camping de l'Aumône
❷ Camping Maison de la Croix
❸ Beach Sailing Club

This is the first port of call after you come off the Greenway. A sleepy stretch of smart cottages opposite the vast bay. This is a place that maximises on the wind: sand yachting is all the rage, even if the long line of windmills on the seafront have long been out of commission.

 **Where to sleep?**

La Croix Galliot, 28 la Croix Galliot. **02 99 48 90 44. la-croix-galliot.fr**. Mme. Taillebois. 5 rooms. €40 single occ. From €47 shared.

Le Lac, 124, Rue du Han. **02 99 48 93 77 or 06 50 57 13 07**. **chambres-cherrueix.fr**. Mme Guitton. 4 rooms from €53 shared. Nice standard of décor.

Where to eat & drink?

L'Abri des Grèves, 2 bis, Rue de la Plage. **02 99 48 99 99**. Bar, restaurant and crêperie on the bay. Great setting. €15-€30.

LE VIVIER-SUR-MER

Route Info

> About 4km beyond Cherrueix, following the road. Be careful as this will be busy in the summer. The presence of boats with aluminium wheels suggests that the harvesting of mussel beds plays a big part here. This stretch of coast up to Cancale is dedicated to seafood production, and oysters play a big part further up the bay. This is a pleasant coastal resort.

 Where to eat & drink?

Hôtel Le Bretagne, 6 Rond Point du Centre. **02 99 80 82 87. hotel-restaurant-le-bretagne.com**. Great location with a dining room overlooking the beach. Simple but splendid seafood. Menus €22-€38.

L'Eveil des Sens, 21 Rue de la Mairie. **02 99 48 90 65**. Menus €19-€26. This is a serious restaurant serving upmarket, super-fresh seafood delights.

L'Amaryllis, 8 Rue Dol. **02 99 48 83 61**. Good line in pizzas. Good use of local produce, too.

 Where to sleep?

£ £ Hôtel Le Bretagne**, 6 Rond Point du Centre, 35960 Le Vivier-sur-Mer. **02 99 80 82 87. hotel-restaurant-le-bretagne.com**. 19 rooms. €59 for shared room. Clean and comfortable.

£ £ Hôtel Restaurant Beau Rivage***, 21 Rue de la Mairie. **02 99 48 90 65. logis-beaurivage.com**. 28 rooms. From €62. A bit a curate's egg, this place. Reviews suggest that not all the rooms are great. Avoid those in the courtyard.

LE VIVIER-SUR-MER TO CANCALE

17km (10.7miles)

Challenge:

Easy. Roads, country lanes.

Route Info

Continue along the coastal road for about 8km after Le Vivier until you arrive in the attractive resort of St-Benoît-des-Ondes. You can carry on along the coast all the way to Cancale or follow the route by heading inland (left!) about 1.5km outside St-Benoît, by the go-karting track. The signs here say they are temporary. The route rises steeply uphill for a brief section before you go left at the cross-roads and up to St-Méloir-des-Ondes.

ST-BENOÎT-DES-ONDES
& ST-MÉLOIR-DES-ONDES

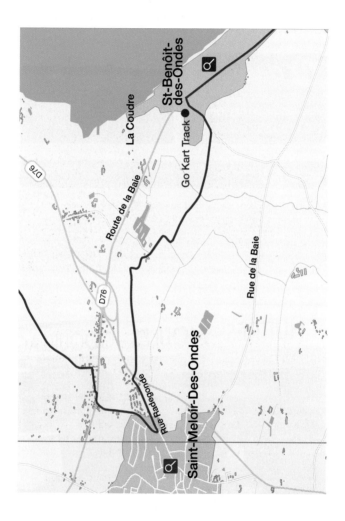

**For accommodation and refreshment purposes we have
lumped the two places together.**

St-Benoît, like Le Vivier and Hirel, was reclaimed from the sea as
long ago as the 11th century with the building of dykes. This created
communities – isolated at high tide – along the rich sandbanks. Fishing
was *the* industry before a tide of tourism changed the demography in
the latter half of the last century. Until World War I nearly half the male
population departed every year for the Grand Banks, off Newfoundland.
Now the coastline is dotted with large oyster farms and mussel beds.

Where to eat & drink?

Jardin du Fruit de Mer, 7 Rue du Bord de Mer, Saint-Benoît-des-
Ondes. **02 99 58 62 15. jardindufruitdemer.com**. This is a shop with a
restaurant. Seafood straight from the sea. Spend as much or as little as
you like, but beware: everything is highly tempting.

♥ La Ferme des Nielles-Ostrea, Les Nielles, 35350 Saint-Meloir-des-
Ondes. **02 99 89 12 21**. Set out like a market: you pick up a basket and
choose your meal. There is a wood-burning oven and an excellent and
good value choice of wines. These upmarket seafood shacks are a great
innovation and a splendid change from all the crêperies.

L'Escapade , 2 Place du Souvenir, 35350 Saint-Meloir-des-Ondes.
02 99 89 19 56. Crêperie and grill. Great reports.

Maison Tirel Guerin, 1 Le Limonay, 35350 Saint-Meloir-des-Ondes. **02 99 89 10 46. tirel-guerin.com**. This is a gastronomic feature and has been for many years. The place has a Michelin star, although the head chef has moved off to Cancale. Menus from €52.

Le Coquillage, D155 Route du Mont-St-Michel, Le Buot, 35350 St-Meloir-des-Ondes. 5km from Cancale. **02 99 89 64 76. maisons-de-bricourt.com**. If you are going to splash out on one fine dining experience during your journey, let it be here: the chef/owner Olivier Roellinger closed down his 3 Michelin star restaurant to concentrate on other aspects of his business and the cooking here reflects that. Fabulous fusion of spices and produce, creating great flavours using local resources. Not for nothing was Roellinger regarded by fellow chefs as the finest in France. Grand Edwardian villa with views from Mont-St-Michel right across the bay. See also hotels. Menus €59-€135.

Where to sleep?

B&B

Le Pont Prin, 35350 Saint-Méloir-des-Ondes. **02 99 89 13 05. tireles-du-pont-prin.com**. Mme Boutier. 3 rooms from €40. €45 sharing. Traditional town house. Barbecue area.

La Ferme du Point du Jour, Le Buot, 35350 Saint-Méloir-des-Ondes. **02 99 89 10 29** or **06 30 03 93 40. fermedupointdujour.com**. Mme Bunouf. 4 rooms. From €40. €55-€57 sharing. Renovated farmhouse in the bay. Covered swimming pool.

Mme Brévault, 14 Rue d'Emeraude, 35350 Saint-Méloir-des-Ondes. **02 99 89 11 78** or **06 62 41 59 86. maureen.ot.cancale@wanadoo.fr**. Family room in separate building. 2 rooms. In the countryside.

Les Portes Rouge, 35350 Saint-Méloir-des-Ondes. **02 99 89 19 52 or 06 73 76 27 42. maureen.ot.cancale@wanadoo.fr**. Mme Pierrette. 4 rooms from €30. €45 sharing. Family rooms. €45 single occ. €45 sharing.

La Seigneurie des Ondes, 35114 Saint-Méloir-des-Ondes. **02 99 58 62 96 or 06 72 43 06 97. la-seigneurie-des-ondes.net.** 18th century manor house with 3 suites. €90-€130 per suite. Spectacular setting near the bay.

HOTELS

💶 Hôtel de la Baie, 6, Rue du Bord de Mer, 35114 Saint-Benôit-des-Ondes. Basic seafront hotel with restaurant. Mixed reviews but great location.

💶💶💶💶 Maison Tirel Guerin****, 1 Le Limonay, 35350 Saint-Méloir-des-Ondes. **02 99 89 10 46. tirel-guerin.com**. Famous for its Michelin-starred restaurant, this is a *hotel de luxe*.

♡ 💶💶💶💶 Chateau Richeux, D155 Route du Mont-St-Michel, Le Buot, 35350 St-Méloir-des-Ondes. 5km from Cancale. 02 99 89 64 76. maisons-de-bricourt.com. This is the hotel which houses Le Coquillage, so if you are going to eat here, you may as well try and book a room. The service is faultless and the rooms are as comfortable as you could wish.

CAMPING

La Ferme du Point du Jour, Pré Vert (Gîtes de France), le Buot, 35350 Saint-Méloir-des-Ondes. **06 30 03 93 40** or **02 99 89 10 29**. **fermedupointdujour.com**. 400m from the bay, they provide 4 B&B rooms and a gîte. €13.60 a night for campers. Great spot.

♡ *La Gouesnière is 4km from St-Méloir and has the excellent but modest Hôtel du Commerce where a room can be had for €52. The restaurant is good and the couple who run it are helpful. **02 99 58 23 06. hotel-cancale.fr.***

Route Info

▶ The rural lane from the coast will shortly cross the busy D76. Take care. The route bears left towards the centre of St-Méloir for a few hundred metres before taking a sharp right for about 500m. Cross the D155 and look out for the little slip road on the other side, which takes you to a T-junction after 150m. Here, go left for 3km before going left again (at the T-junction with the C2). Continue for a further 2.5km, then go right into St-Coulomb.

Route to Cancale

▶ At the T-junction with the C2 (at Les Hauts Champs), instead of going left to St-Coulomb, head right for Cancale. To enjoy the best route take the 2nd right after 700m. After a kilometre or so you will sweep sharply round to the left going downhill towards the seafront. Enjoy the views. A circular route takes you back out of Cancale at the far end of the Port de la Houle.

CANCALE

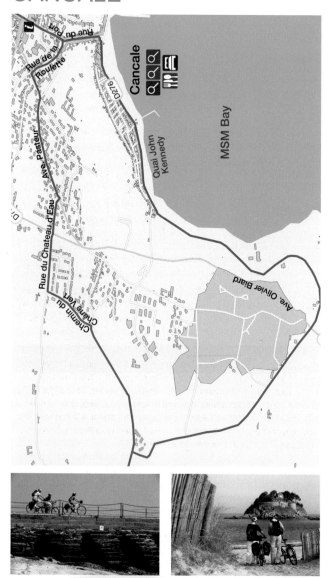

Welcome to Crustacean Central, the mollusc capital of Brittany. Cancale lives, eats and breathes shellfish thanks to a 15-metre tide that makes it ideal for cultivating them. The Atlantic flushes through the Bay of Mont-Saint-Michel, producing one of the biggest tides in Europe, and makes for a dramatically varying coastline as it ebbs and flows. It also means that the water is clean and the beaches daily scrubbed by the sea itself. Cancale is a town of two halves. Up top is the old bit, with the ancient Eglise St-Méen, named after the Welsh saint who settled in the 6th century and whose church houses the Musée des Arts et Traditions Populaires. Here upmarket seaside villas and large townhouses reflect the wealth of locals and holiday homeowners alike. The ostréiculteurs sell 25,000 tonnes of the hard-shelled bivalve every year and a large proportion are consumed at the 90 or so restaurants in the area.

Down below is the old port, La Houle, where fishermen's cottages are packed together in a charming and colourful huddle. The seafront is all restaurants, hotels and bars, many of them very good. Those who enjoy cooking and who fancy hanging around for a day or two, should enrol on one of Olivier Roellinger's cooking classes. Roellinger is a former 3-star Michelin chef and is to Cancale what Rick Stein is to Padstow, except with significantly more kitchen firepower.

This part of Brittany is reminiscent of North Cornwall, with its cliffs, creeks and headlands that disappear into the boiling ocean. To the east lies a vast expanse of sand and marsh and every morning the sun rises over Mont-Saint-Michel as the fishing boats potter around in the bay. 'For the past 500 years they were all cod fishermen,' says Roellinger, who hung up is tocque to concentrate on his wider business. 'Until the early 20th century nearly all of the boats in Cancale and Saint-Malo were bound for Newfoundland and they were all handmade by local craftsmen.'

Nearly all the restaurants here specialise in seafood. The prices mentioned are mostly from menus but you can spend more if you wish by going à la carte.

 Where to eat & drink?

L'Ormeau, 4 Quai Thomas, 35260 Cancale. **02 99 89 60 16. restaurant-ormeau-cancale.fr**. Ormeau means abalone. At the end of the quay, elegant wood panelling and views of the harbour. Seafood's the theme. Menus from €21 to €72.

La Maison de la Marine, 23 Rue de la Marine, 35260 Cancale. **02 99 89 88 53. maisondelamarine.com**. Former maritime centre done out comfortably. Good modern cuisine at a reasonable price. Menus from €27. Tasting menu €69.

Le Surcouf, 7 Quai Gambetta, 35260 Cancale. **02 99 89 61 75**. Formulaic seafood staples well executed. Ravioli of langoustine and planchas of fish. Good views and reasonable prices: menus from €14 to €44.

Breizh Café, 7 Quai Thomas, 35260 Cancale. **02 99 89 61 76. breizhcafe.com**. Bertrand Larcher exported the omnipresent crêpe to Japan, and imported the Japanese restaurant to Brittany. Great crêpes and superb Japanese restaurant upstairs (see below). Menus €14 to €34. There's a Breizh Café in Paris and Tokyo, too.

♥ La Table de Breizh Café, 7 Quai Thomas, 35260 Cancale. **02 99 89 61 76. breizhcafe.com**. This is the best of Japan meeting the finest Breton produce. Two evening tasting menus come at Tokyo prices: €60 and €120. Tempura of lobster with razor clams in a jus of white skipjack. Fine fusion cooking with reasonable lunchtime menus from €38.

♥ Le Troquet, 19 Quai Gambetta, 35260 Cancale. **02 99 89 99 42**. Fine seafood at reasonable prices on the seafront. This is probably euro for euro the best place in Cancale, with super-fresh seafood alongside such dishes as pig cheek shepherd's pie. Good wine cellar. Menus from €18 to €38.

♥ Le Querrien, 7 Quai Duguay-Trouin, 35260 Cancale. **02 99 89 64 56. le-querrien.com**. Highly rated and amusingly nautical restaurant with rooms. Terrace with view over bay and affordable prices. Menus from €15 (weekdays) to €32.

♥ Côté Mer, Route de la Corniche, 35260 Cancale. **02 99 89 66 08**. **restaurant-cotemer.fr.** Guillaume Tirrel, the Michelin-starred chef from the Maison Tirel Guerin at St-Méloir has taken over here and elevated the cooking to the highest levels. At the end of the long seafront stretch. Menus €27 to €46.

La Pointe du Grouin, 35260 Pointe du Grouin. 6km from Cancale. **02 99 89 60 55. hotelpointedugrouin.com**. Unbeatable location near the 'end of the earth' with views to match. Traditional and well executed cooking. Menus from €24.

♥ Le Bénétin, Chemin des Rochers-Sculptés, 35400 Rothéneuf. **02 99 56 97 64. restaurant-lebenetin.com**. 5km before you get to St-Malo lies this large, charming and well run restaurant with its stunning sea view terrace. Usually packed (with locals); you definitely need to book. Young chef with fresh ideas. Menus from €25.

🛏 Where to sleep?

HOTELS

♥  Hôtel Duguay Trouin***, 11 Quai Duguay Trouin, 35260 Cancale. **02 23 15 12 07. hotelduguaytrouin.com**. 7 rooms from €95 to €115. Well run and charming, right on the bay. One of the best in the area.

£ £ Hôtel Nuit et Jour**, 3 Avenue de Scissy, 35260 Cancale. **02 99 89 75 59. hotel-nuitetjour.com**. 30 rooms from €58 to €73. In the middle of a park 1km from centre of Cancale. Swimming pool and fitness centre.

£ £/£ £ £ Hôtel-Restaurant Le Champlain***, 1, Quai Administrateur Thomas, 35260 Cancale. **02 99 89 60 04. lamerechamplain.com**. 17 rooms from €69 to €169. Completely renovated.

£ £/£ £ £ Hôtel-Restaurant Le Querrien, 7 Quai Duguay Trouin, 35260 Cancale. **02 99 89 64 56. le-querrien.com**. 16 rooms from €53 to €144. Rooms above a noted restaurant with good half-board details (see website).

£ £ Hôtel-Restaurant de la Plage, 11 Rue Eugène et Auguste Feyen Port Mer, 35260 Cancale. **02 99 89 81 59. hoteldelaplage-cancale**. com. 8 rooms, one of which will take 5. €89. Non-classified. Restaurant overlooking the beach.

£ £ £ La Maison de la Marine, 23 Rue de la Marine, 35260 Cancale. **02 99 89 88 53. maisondelamarine.com**. Weekend offers DB&B for 2 €180. 5 rooms. Very stylish.

£ £ £ La Pointe du Grouin***, 35260 Pointe du Grouin. 6km miles from Cancale. **02 99 89 60 55. hotelpointedugrouin.com**. All rooms have sea views. Tastefully decorated. The Pointe de Grouin is the NW tip of the peninsula 6km from Cancale. 15 rooms from €88 to €160. Deals possible for half-board.

B&B

Mme Cadiou, 99 bis, Rue du Verger, Cancale 35260. **02 99 89 70 01. gitesdefrance35.com**. 3 rooms from €50 single occ or €52 to €58 for 2 or from €65 for 3. Renovated farmhouse.

La Maison de la Marine, 23 Rue de la Marine, 35260 Cancale. **02 99 89 88 53. maisondelamarine.com**. 7 rooms. Upmarket (and expensive). From €80 for 1 to €160.

Le Victor Hugo, 20 Rue Victor Hugo, 35260 Cancale. **02 99 89 92 81. le-victor-hugo.com**. 5 rooms from €54. 2 people €70 to €70. Old fisherman's house down in the port.

Mme Lebel, 6 Avenue de la Cote d'Emeraude, 35260 Cancale. **02 99 89 67 01. maureen.ot.cancale@wanadoo.fr**. 3 rooms €55 for 2 (same for 1) and €65 for 3 sharing.

CAMPING

Les Clos Fleuris, La Ville es Poulains, 35260 Cancale. **02 99 89 97 68. cancale-campings.fr**. 11 pitches. €16 for 2.

Camping Nôtre Dame du Verger, Le Verger, 35260 Cancale. **02 99 89 72 84. camping-verger.com**. 22 hectares 400m from sea. Check website for details.

Camping Municipal de la Pointe de Grouin, La Pointe du Grouin, 35260 Cancale. **02 99 89 63 79** or **02 99 89 60 15. campingcancale@orange.fr**. 199 pitches, great location.

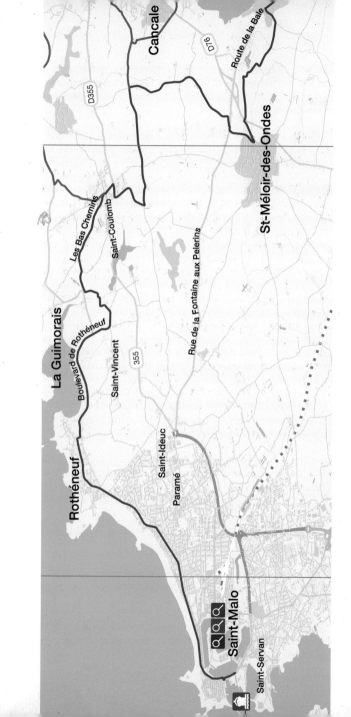

CANCALE TO SAINT-MALO

15.6km (9.8miles)

Challenge:
Easy. Quiet lanes then cycle lane into St-Malo.

Route Info

At the end of the Quai Duguay Trouin, at the Hôtel Mère Champlain, go up the Rue du Port taking the first left, onto the Rue de la Roulette. 300m and head left along the D76 (Avenue Pasteur); go right onto the Rue Cháteau d'Eau and cross the D201 before heading left on the Chemin du Chêne Vert to rejoin the route to St-Coulomb.

Alternatively, head right along the D201 (Avenue de Scissy) and up to the Pointe de Grouin. This is a bit of a diversion, but well worth it for experienced cyclists (there is likely to be traffic). The D201 follows the northern tip of the Emerald Peninsula, taking you alongside some fine, long stretches of sand. This route is very popular with local cyclists. (see map below)

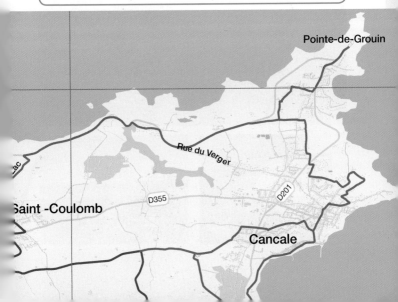

◗ After roughly 2.5km, having crossed the D74, go right at the crossroads (this is signposted) and the lane will bring you down into St-Coulomb.

Route from Saint-Coulomb

◗ Follow signs taking you left onto the Grand Rue de la Poste then head right onto the D74 Place de l'Eglise for 50m before taking the next left onto the Rue de la Mairie, heading out of town and up to the crossroads (1.3km) where you head left for 600m before going left again at the T-junction. This scenic wiggle brings you out on the D201 which you now follow, through the pleasant seaside resort of Rothéneuf, and into the outskirts of St-Malo.

◗ The Boulevard Rothéneuf becomes the Boulevard John Kennedy and you approach the walled intramuros citadel of St-Malo through the suburb of Paramé, a vast sandy expanse for now (irritatingly) hidden by the back ends of endless hotels and smart holiday villas. You hit the seafront (on your right!) about 1km short of the walled city.

◗ Continue past the car parks and the ferry terminus is just beyond the walls, well signposted, after two bridges which separate the Bassin Vauban from the Channel.

SAINT-MALO

This grey granite fortress was built on the profits of piracy and trade. Buccaneering corsairs held the Channel to ransom with such success that at one point St-Malo held 25% of France's gold reserves. Louis XIV, no less, came on bended knee for loans. This is reflected in its architecture: the townscape positively swaggers, even to this day, paid for in part by English shipping bagged in La Manche.

The citadel – known as *intra-muros* – became a key port in the 17th and 18th centuries, when it was separated from the mainland. Its privateers were government sanctioned to discourage the English from similar activities (see Dorset chapter: Poole).

Though largely destroyed in August 1944, St-Malo was lovingly restored to its former state, much as Warsaw was post WWII, and later, Dubrovnik, after the Croatian War of Independence. You would not be aware that the Allied bombers, who wrecked St-Lô, Vire and much of Normandy, had been anywhere near.

St-Malo is the most popular tourist resort in Brittany. Its narrow cobbled streets, hewn from the same stone as Mont-Saint-Michel, heave with high-class boutiques, bars, restaurants and hotels. This place does chic as well as catering for the masses, and somehow carries it off, despite its relatively cramped quarters. One of the draws is its magisterial Atlantic vistas. Another, its sandy beaches and labyrinth of passageways behind the 6-metre thick walls designed by the great French military engineer, Vauban.

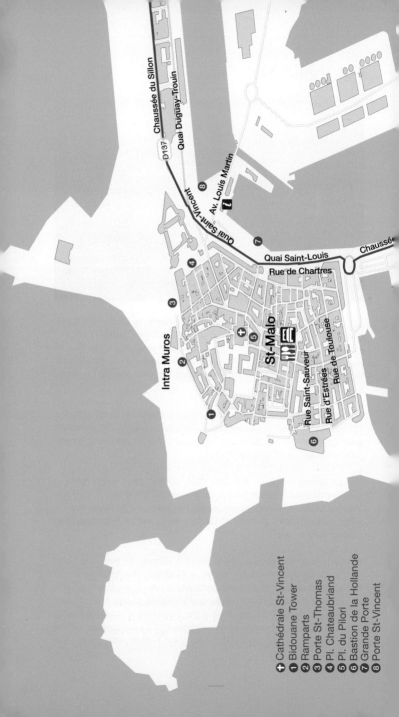

Chaussée du Sillon
D137
Quai Duguay-Trouin
Quai Saint-Vincent
Av. Louis Martin

8

Quai Saint-Louis
Rue de Chartres

7

4
3

Intra Muros

St-Malo

2
5

Rue Saint-Sauveur
Rue d'Estrées
Rue de Toulouse

1

6

Chaussé

✚ Cathédrale St-Vincent
❶ Bidouane Tower
❷ Ramparts
❸ Porte St-Thomas
❹ Pl. Chateaubriand
❺ Pl. du Pilori
❻ Bastion de la Hollande
❼ Grande Porte
❽ Porte St-Vincent

As for the seafood...

 Where to eat & drink?

INTRA MUROS (INSIDE THE WALLS)

L'Eveil des Sens, 6 Rue Ste-Barbe. **02 99 40 92 46. leveildessens. fr**. Opened in June 2012 and you will need to book if you want to eat Yannick Lalande's food. Rave reports from all quarters. We were unable to secure a table, so missed the pumpkin soup with foie gras, oyster tartare with scallops, pink veal kidneys and tarte tatin. Michelin fame predicted. Menus from €25.

Le Bistro de Jean, 6 Rue de la Corne-de-Cerf. **02 99 40 98 68**. A quintessential upmarket French bistro, accomplished bourgeois cooking and friendly service. Big portions, deep flavours, traditional style. There used to be lots of places like this in France. Menus from €14. Very reasonably priced.

La Brasserie Armoricaine, 6 Rue du Boyer. **02 99 40 89 13. hotel-armoricaine.com**. Perfectly preserved in aspic, a 1950s time warp. You could imagine comic actor Jacques Tati lurching through the door with his tennis racket. Traditional French cooking heavily accented towards seafood (there's an aquarium full of lobsters in the middle of the room). Amazingly good value, with a solid and affordable wine list. Great service. From €14.

Le Chalut, 8 Rue de la Corne-de-Cerf. **02 99 56 71 58. lechalutstmalo@aol.com**. Michelin starred cooking in a nautical setting – art decko? – this is *the* place for lobster. Sophisticated, upmarket and reassuringly expensive, it's next door to Le Bistro de Jean. Menus €25 to €70.

La Coquille d'Oeuf, 20 Rue de la Corne-de-Cerf. **02 99 40 92 62. lucette-dechaume@orange.fr**. Everything is cooked from scratch by the chef-proprietor: he does his own foie gras, smokes his own salmon etc. Splendid little place, cosy and warm. €25 to €35.

Tanpopo, 5 place Poissonnerie. **02 99 40 87 53. tanpopo-stmalo. fr**. Real Japanese 'home' cooking: evenings offer 7 course set menus which take 2.5 to 3 hours. Sashimi of sardine with foie gras in aspic, pork burger with whelk fritters and seaweed pancake, a crab-in-jelly soup made with the leaves of a cherry tree, and veal and oyster strudels. This is art. Menus €21 for lunch; €41 for dinner. You need to book as it is understandably popular.

Côté Sens, 16 Rue de la Herse. **02 99 20 08 12. cote-sens.com.** Well run, small and good traditional cooking. €28 to €45.

L'Ancrage, 7 Rue J. Cartier. **02 99 40 15 97.** Up on the ramparts with great views, it's boat-themed from beam to bowsprit and a good spot to weigh anchor if Neptune's harvest is your thing. Nautical but nice. From €16.

Crêperie-la-Brigantine, 13 Rue de Dinan. **02 99 56 82 82. creperielabrigantine@orange.fr.** It would be a shame not to single out a crêperie in this capital of crêpes. This one does a whole range, from offal to cheese to apple flambéed with calvados. You can get one for €8.

OUTSIDE THE WALLS

Le Saint-Placide, 6 Place du Poncel. **02 99 81 70 73. st-placide.com.** Discreetly tucked away beyond the ferry terminal in the old tramway station, this is reckoned by many to be the top table in Saint-Malo. It has a Michelin star and a rave review in Gault & Millau, the French foodie's real bible. Local produce from lobster to lamb cooked with great panache by Luc Mobihan. €27 (lunch). Menus €44 to €130.

La Brasserie du Sillon, 3 Chaussée du Sillon. **02 99 56 10 74.** Pretty much on the beach and a 10 minute walk from the ramparts. Good value, professional outlet. Plenty of seats and usually busy. From €17 to €62.

La Corderie, 9 Chemin de la Corderie. **02 99 81 62 38.** Close to the ferry port in a manor house overlooking the bay. Lovely terrace and exotic seafood cooking, using spices imaginatively. Good service and reasonably priced. €17 to €43.

Where to sleep?

INTRA MUROS (INSIDE THE WALLS)

Le Quic en Groigne**, 8 Rue d'Estrées. **02 99 20 22 20. quic-en-groigne.com.** Small hotel tucked away in a quiet street. Accommodating, friendly and very well run. Tremendous value.

Hôtel-Brasserie Armoricaine, 6 Rue du Boyer. **02 99 40 89 13. hotel-armoricaine.com.** Old-fashioned and low budget hotel in one of the less hectic quarters. If you stay, you should also eat at its restaurant.

£ £ Central, 6 Grande Rue. **02 99 40 87 70. bestwestern-hotelcentral-saintmalo.com**. 50 rooms. Seafood restaurant nautically themed.

£ £ Hôtel de la Cité***, 26 Rue Ste-Barbe. **02 99 40 10 04. hotelcite.com**. 41 rooms. Sea views, comfortable and well run.

£ £ San Pedro, 1 Rue Ste-Anne. **02 99 40 88 57**. Close to the Bon Secours beach. 12 rooms. Renowned for its friendly service, according to the Michelin Guide Rouge. 'Tiny but perfectly maintained rooms. Impeccable breakfast.'

£ £ Le Croiseur**, 2 Place de la Poissonnerie. **02 99 40 80 40. hotel-le-croiseur.com**. 14 rooms. Trendy minimalist set-up serving breakfast in the cobbled courtyard, weather permitting.

£ £ £ Ajoncs d'Or, 10 Rue Forgeurs. **02 99 40 85 03. st-malo-hotel-ajoncs-dor.com**. Striking maritime themes. 22 rooms in a quiet side street.

£ £ £ Hôtel du Louvre, 2 Rue Marins. **02 99 40 86. hoteldulouvre-saintmalo.com**. Completely and tastefully renovated. 50 rooms.

£ £ £ France & Chateaubriand***, 12 Place Châteaubriand. **02 99 56 66 52. hotel-chateaubriand-st-malo.com**. 80 rooms, 3 restaurants, splendid bar. This is a fine and well run establishment hard by the principal entrance.

OUTSIDE THE WALLS

£ £ La Grassinais**, 12 Allée Grassinais. **02 99 81 33 00**. It may be in a retail park but this hotel has a following. Its restaurant is excellent and the hotel is well managed and good value for money.

£ £/£ £ £ Le Kyriad***, 49 Chaussée du Sillon. **02 99 56 09 26. kyriadsaintmaloplage.com**. Bang on the beach 1km from the ramparts and 500m from the *thalasso* baths. 56 rooms.

£ £/£ £ £ Hôtel Mercure, 36 Chaussée du Sillon. **02 23 18 47 47. accorhotels.com**. Formulaic set-up but run with charm. Overlooks the beach and good deals possible.

£ £ £ Hôtel Beaufort, 25 Chaussée du Sillon. **02 99 40 99 99. hotel-beaufort.com**. This grand old lady was built as the luxury seaside villa of an Egyptian aristocrat in 1860. Nice restful spot, handy for taking the waters.

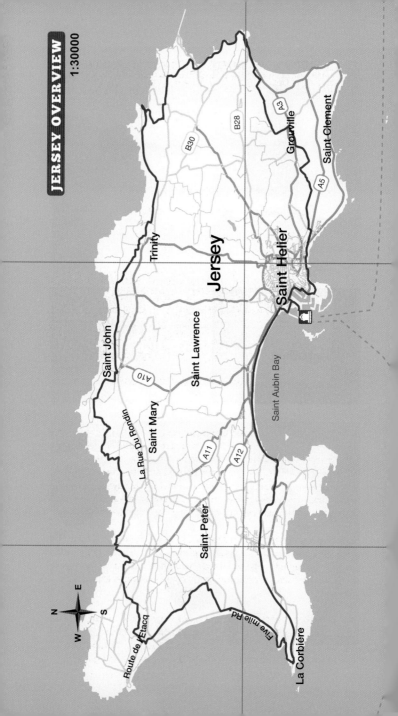

JERSEY 65km (40.6miles)

ST HELIER TO ST HELIER

St Helier > La Corbière = 12.1km (7.6miles)
La Corbière > St John = 19.1km (12miles)
St John > Grouville = 26.4km (16.5miles)
Grouville > St Helier = 7.4km (4.6miles)

Challenge:

Easy to moderate. Occasional climbing. Mostly on quiet lanes with one stretch off-road (though you can take the road instead if on a road bike).

*THIS ROUTE IS DESCRIBED CLOCKWISE.

ST HELIER

14km wide and 8km top to bottom, Jersey has some of the best beaches in the world, as good for surfing as it is for sandcastles. It is also studded with some marvellous fortresses which somehow add a note of glamour and threat to the ordered calm of island life. The weather is temperate and the scenery stunning, with vast sandy bays and 10m tidal movements which reveal a vast rock-strewn sandscape at low tide. On the right day, the beaches have a positively Caribbean feel to them.

St Helier has some fine old fashioned and some superb restaurants. The latter are scattered liberally around the island as this is truly a gourmet's paradise. There may be a connection here with it being a tax exile's paradise, as such folk can afford to eat out regularly and expect high standards.

Jersey has a feel of 1950s England about it, apart from the smart glass towers and pin stripes in its city district. The Channel Islands, of which it is the largest, are the last remants of the Dukedom of Normandy, and are under separate jurisdiction from the UK. Jersey is a self-governing

147

British Crown dependency and, as such, is not administered by the UK.

During the 1980s it featured weekly on British TV as the setting for the hit detective series, Bergerac. It was also the only part of Britain to be invaded by the Germans in World War II, but following Bergerac it was invaded once again, this time by tourists.

Apart from tourism (24% of GDP), banking and finance (60% of GDP) and a splendid climate, Jersey is renowned for agriculture. Produce includes potatoes (Jersey Royals), cauliflower, tomatoes, flowers, beef and dairy produce.

Eating

Jersey is also renowned for its excellent restaurants. There are many French, Italian and Portuguese restaurants. There are occasionally themed 'food weeks' celebrating the different cultures on the Island. Every October (for a little over a month) is the 'Tennerfest' when you can eat in many of the world-class restaurants, including Michelin starred-ones, from around £10 (hence Tennerfest).

Drinking

Despite little duty on alcohol you pay London prices in pubs and clubs. Normal pub closing time is 11pm and most clubs have to be closed by 2am (there is no 'drinking-up-time'). There are a few bars with alfresco areas including one with a view over the bay toward Elizabeth Castle. Most of the working-men's pubs became trendy wine bars in the early nineties so there's not much chance of finding a pool table in town.

The main town of St. Helier is compact enough that you can wander from pub to pub and club to club quite easily.

*PLACES IN JERSEY HAVE UK DIALLING CODES (+44).

Worth a visit: **Jersey War Tunnels**, Les Charrières Malorey, St Lawrence, Jersey, JE3 1FU. Head west from St Helier taking the inner main road. From Bel Royal the attraction is well signposted. 01534 860808. jerseywartunnels.com. 10:00-18:00. Formerly known as the German Underground Hospital, the tunnels were built during the Second World War, and now are an interesting tourist attraction. Cut deeply into rising hills, the site is now a museum telling the story of Jersey, which, along with the other Channel Islands, was the only part of Britain to be occupied by Germany during the war. £10.50.

The Durrell Wildlife Conservation Trust, durrell.org.

The Eric Young Orchid Foundation, ericyoungorchidfoundation.co.uk.

Mont Orgueil Castle, jerseyheritage.org. This mighty bastion dominates the local skyline and is well worth a visit.

▶ GETTING THERE

By Air

Jersey Airport is in the parish of St. Peter. Air France, Flybe, Easyjet, British Airways, and Aurigny Airlines offer regular flights from London (Gatwick, Stansted and Luton) and other airports of Great Britain. Aer Lingus offers regular flights from Dublin, Ireland. There are also regular flights to Switzerland (provided by local airline Blueislands) and seasonal flights from Dusseldorf with Air Berlin.

By Ferry

But you will most probably be coming by boat from St-Malo via Condor Ferries. condorferries.co.uk.

UK: 01202 207216
Jersey: 01534 872240
Guernsey: 12023 (local calls only)
St. Malo: 0825 165 463
Cherbourg: +33 2 33 88 44 88

Languages

English is the official everyday tongue.
French is occasionally used by officialdom.
Jèrriais is the local Norman patois, spoken mainly in country districts.
Portuguese is also widely spoken.

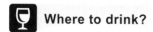 **Where to drink?**

Admiral, 12 & 14 St. James Street, St Helier JE2 3QZ. 01534 730095. Open all day. Big, bustling pub serving food. Lively at weekends. Shows sport.

Cock & Bottle, Halkett Place, St Helier JE2 4WG. 01534 722184. Lovely old pub with a big terrace in Royal Square, right in the centre. Food served.

Lamplighter, Mulcaster St, St Helier JE2 3NJ. 01534 723119. Has largest selection of real ales on the island. Busy and full of character. Town centre. Food served.

The Wharf Bar, The Wharf, St Helier JE1 3UF. 01534 880110. Part of the Pomme d'Or Hotel, a popular centrally located bar. Food served.

Post Horn, Hue Street, St. Helier JE2 3RE. 01534 872853. In the heart of the city centre, near all the shops, the Post Horn is a locals' pub with a large al fresco eating and drinking area, which is a sun trap. Food served and open all day. Free wifi and local ales on tap.

 Where to eat?

The Sirocco, Royal Yacht Hotel, Caledonia Place, Weighbridge, St Helier JE2 3NF. 01534 720511. theroyalyacht.com. Good restaurant at the famous hotel. Also under the same roof: Café Zephyr and The Grill. Modern British cuisine at the sophisticated Sirocco to more basic, but well executed Grill.

Park House, 1 La Colomberie, St Helier, JE2 4QH. 01534 874196. Popular town centre Thai restaurant.

Doran's Courtyard Bistro, Kensington Place, St Helier, JE2 3PA. 01534 734866. jerseyrooms.co.uk. Oak beams and flagstone floors. Mediterranean-Moorish leanings.

The Inn Boutique, Queens Road, St Helier. 01534 722239. theinnjersey.com. Restaurant with rooms, highly rated and vegetarian options get rave reviews. About £30 for 3 courses.

Green Olive, 1 Anley St, St Helier' JE2 3QE. 01534 728198. greenoliverestaurant.co.uk. Asian fusion cooking of a very high order combined with some imaginative Modern British takes. Amazingly good value given the level of cuisine. Asian spiced duck confit with udon noodles is good, as are haddock fish fingers in a tempura batter, triple cooked chips with mushy peas and tartare sauce. £ for £ the best in St Helier.

Indian Ocean, 37 La Motte St, St Helier JE2 4SZ. 01534 766118. indianocean.je. Great feedback on this cheap and cheerful Indian smack in the centre of town. All the usual dishes.

Wildfire Tapas & Bars, 14 Mulcaster Street, Opposite the Royal Yacht Hotel, St Helier JE2 3NJ. 01534 625555. Steaks and tapas are highly praised. Healthy portions well executed. You'll spend anywhere between £15 and £30 on food.

The Dicq Slip, St Saviour, JE2 7PD. 01534 730273. On a hot day this is a great place for Thai food. BYOB (there's a shop opposite). The longest serving Thai establishment in Jersey and extremely popular. Casual, no bookings, food cooked on beach. Picnic benches. Reckoned to be the best of the island's excellent Thai establishments. A short distance east of centre, near the golf course.

Bastille Brasserie, 35 Queen Street, St Helier, Jersey, JE2 4WD. 01534 874059. A little French Brasserie in the Heart of St Helier serving authentic French food. Wine bar at the front serving snacks with full restaurant at the rear.

Prince of Wales Tavern, 'French Lane', Hilgrove Lane, St Helier, JE2 4SL 01534 737378. Lovely old pub with a beautiful (and hidden) beer garden in the middle of town next to the wonderful Victorian covered markets.

Bohemia, Green St, Saint Helier JE2 4UH. 01534 880588. bohemiajersey.com. Menu: £25/£85. Steep? Yes, but this is a very fine restaurant indeed and if you want to treat yourself, it's arguably the best on the island. Classically based cooking with modern twists. Try ox cheek and cod. Or anything, for that matter.

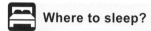 **Where to sleep?**

£ £ £ Eulah Country House Hotel*****, Mont Cochon, St Helier JE2 3JA. **01534 626626. eulah.co.uk**. Between St. Helier and St. Lawrence, this elegant 7 room Edwardian pile won the 2013 Tripadvisor Travellers' Choice award and scores maximum points. Pound for pound, probably the top spot on the island. Pool, gym and many extras.

£ £/£ £ £ £ Radisson Blu Waterfront****, Rue de l'Etau, St Helier, JE2 3WF. **01534 671100. radissonblu.co.uk/hotel-jersey**. 195 rooms. You can get a deal (from £60) with advanced booking. Spectacular views.

£ £ £ £ The Royal Yacht Hotel****, Caledonia Place, Weighbridge, St Helier JE2 3NF. **01534 720511. theroyalyacht.com**. Great situation but limited views. Spa and luxury.

B&B

£ Surrey Lodge Guest House,20 Belmont Road, St Helier JE2 4SA. **01534 734834. surreylodge.com**. Highly recommended. Cheap, friendly and comfortable.

£ Kensington Guest House, 21, Kensington Place, St Helier. **01534 732827. kensingtonguesthouse.com**. 12 rooms. Ideal for a cyling group. Right in the centre with restaurants and bars nearby.

£ Jaylana Guest Accommodation, La Route de St Aubin, First Tower, St Helier JE2 3LN. **01534 731 877. jaylanaguesthouse.co.uk**. Comfortable, clean and 5 minutes from the centre.

£ £ La Bonne Vie Guest House, Roseville Street, St Helier JE2 4PL. **01534 735955. labonnevieguesthousejersey.com**. Slap in the town centre, smart and comfortable.

£ £/£ £ £ Bay View Guest House, 12 Havre des Pas, St Helier, JE2 4UQ. **01534 720950. bayviewjersey.com**. AA 4-star and top notch but a bit pricey.

CAMPSITE

Beuvelande Camp Site, Rue de Beuvelande, St Martin JE3 6EF. About 5 miles north east of St. Helier. **01534 853575. campingjersey.com**. Outdoor heated pool, food, entertainment and bar. Highly recommended.

OUT OF TOWN HOTELS AND B&BS

Harbour View Guest House, St Aubin's Harbour, St Brelade, JE3 8AB, **01534741585. harbourview@localdial.com**

Villa D'Oro B&B (Cyclists Welcome scheme) La Grande Route de St Laurent, St Lawrence, JE3 1NJ, **01534 862262. stay@villadorojersey.com**

Merton Hotel (Cyclists Welcome scheme), Belvedere, St Saviour, JE4 9PG, **01534 724231. enquiries@mertonhotel.com**

ST HELIER TO LA CORBIÉRE

12.1km (7.6miles)

Challenge: Easy

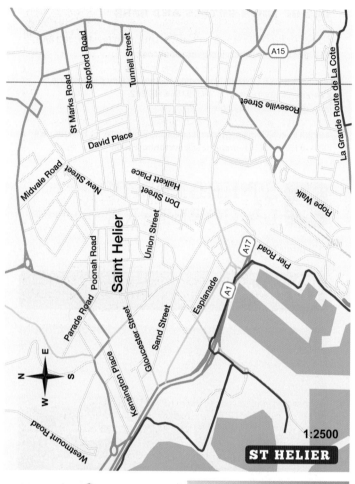

Route Info

▶ Off the ferry, follow the cycle path and the route takes you close to the Radisson and left onto the cycle lane following the coast, westwards, parallel with the A1 around the wide sweep of St Aubin Bay.

▶ Just before you get to St Aubin's Harbour View the path goes off to the right. Keep your eyes open for PTM signs. The route follows the old Jersey Tracks of Steam – known now as Railway Walk, a delightful shaded path.

▶ If you wish to come off and visit the wonderful St Brelade's Bay, depart the Greenway at La Route des Quennevais and go through St Brelade before hitting the wide sandy bay. There are some great places to stop for a meal here. The old rail line continues the short distance to La Corbière.

▶ Look out for the scupture commemorating the rescue of 300 passengers from a French vessel, the St-Malo, in 1995. This is a particularly treacherous stretch of sea, hence La Corbière lighthouse, which witnesses some of the fastest tides in the Channel.

 ## History

La Corbière was formerly the western terminus of the Jersey Railway line from Saint Helier. The first through train ran on 5th August 1885 but the service was ceased in 1935, unable to compete with the new buses. In 1937 a trail now known as the Railway Walk or Tracks of Steam, linking La Corbière and Saint Aubin, for pedestrians and cyclists was opened. During the German occupation 1940-1945, light railways were re-established by the Germans for the purpose of supplying coastal fortifications. A one-metre gauge line was laid down following the route of the former Jersey Railway from Saint Helier to La Corbière, with a branch line connecting the stone quarry at Ronez in Saint John. It was dismantled but other German fortifications remain and can be seen around the headland.

Where to eat?

♥ **Oyster Box Beach Bar & Restaurant**, St Brelade's Bay JE3 8EF. 01534 743311. oysterbox.co.uk. Great seafood in a cool, relaxed setting. Good wine list and relaxing spot for a well earned (but not cheap) lunch.

Crab Shack, St Brelade's Bay JE3 8EF. 01534 744611. crabshackjersey.co.uk. Anything from snacks to a huge *fruits de mer*. Relaxed and informal with lovely terrace. You can spend as much or as little as you like and prices are reasonable.

Le Braye, La Grand Route des Mielles, St Brelade, JE3 8FN 01534 481395. Boules and frites. Fresh local produce, good house wines from Gascony.

Just round the headland at La Pulente on south side of St Ouen's Bay.

Ocean Restaurant, Atlantic Hotel, Le Mont de la Pulente, Jersey, St Brelade JE3 8HE 01534 744101. Michelin-starred, impeccable. Unlikely place for a sweaty cyclist but worth delving into the saddle bag for a shirt and trousers if you feel like pushing the boat out. Great ingredients cooked with panche.

El Tico Beach Cantina, La Grande Route de Mielle, St Peter JE3 7FN. 01534 482009. elticojersey.com. Opposite the golf course and on the beach. Relaxed place to watch the surfers. Almost halfway up St Ouen's Bay. Coffee, snacks or a big meal. Cooking is excellent and seafood fresh as you could want.

LA CORBIÉRE TO ST JOHN

19.1km (12miles)

Challenge: Easy to intermediate (a couple of brief off-road options)

Route Info

● The signage is pretty good for this route. You can also get a detailed local map. The route instructions here are fairly complex as this charming circuit hops from minor road to minor road with great frequency.

● Follow the B44 road round the headland. You can either continue along the road, heading inland 1km or so before bearing left on the B35, known locally as Five Mile Road, and back to the coast. Or you can go off-road and enjoy the views for a brief stretch before pitching up again on the coastal road. After 4km go right onto the Route de la Marette. The road dog-legs after 1km. At the crossroads go left onto the Route de Val de la Mare.

● After about 4km you cross the B35 Five Mile Road, going onto the Chemin de la Brecquette for 300m or so before going right and once again crossing the B35 to head up Mont Vibert. The route is sinuous but well signed.

● You cross the B34 and B55 before heading sharp left ont the Mont de la Grève de Lecq which takes you once again to the shoreline. Here you go briefly off-road up a sharp but brief hill before being reconnected with le Chemin de Catel.

● Follow the coast road as far as the village of St John.

ST JOHNS TO GROUVILLE

26.4km (16.5miles)

Challenge: Easy to intermediate

Route Info

▶ Take the Rue de l'Eglise out of the village. After about 500m a pathway connects Ruette de la Carrière with the Rue de la Mare des Prés. At the next junction bear right onto the Rue de la Petite Lande and continue to the T-junction, where you turn right onto the Rue de Cambrai. Continue for a short distance then head left, crossing the Rue du Tas de Géon onto the Rue de la Bergerie. Continue down the Rue des Fontaines to the T-junction with the Rue de la Petite Falaise, where you go left, right and left again onto the Chemin Olivet.

▶ After just over 1km go left onto the Rue des Côtes du Nord. This takes you to Rozel Bay, briefly inland again along La Vallée de Rozel before clipping Flicquet Bay. Follow signs down to the Rue de la Perruque, which becomes the Rue de Fliquet. At the T-junction head left onto Le Grand Cotil, back towards the coast again.

▶ Go right at the next crossroads onto the Le Mont de la Mare Catherine. Look out for a sharp right turn onto the Rue des Charrières which becomes the Rue de la Forge and the Rue des Vallées before crossing the main road to take La Longue Rue before a sharp left onto the Rue de l'Orme. At the T-junction go left onto the Rue de Beuvelande then right onto the Rue du Bouillon. This will take you back down to the coast near Gorey, where you head sharp right on the La Route de la Cote before going through a couple of hairpins and onto the Gorey Coast Road.

▶ Take the next right up Beach Rd, left at the T-junction then right onto Rue Horman, left onto the Chemin des Maltières and follow the route down to Grouville.

GROUVILLE TO ST HELIER

7.4km (4.6miles)

e Challenge: Easy

Route Info

▶ Leave Grouville on the Rue des Alleurs and head left on the Rue Au Blancq. Go right on Les Huriaux then left on La Rue Solas (into the Rue du Coin) then right onto La Blinerie Lane, skirting the edge of St Clement Golf Course. After the tennis courts, go left onto the Plat Douet Road then left on Green Rd. At the end of Green Road, turn right and follow the shoreline.

▶ Keep your eyes open for the cycle lane, which peels off to the left some 300m after the traffic island, along the edge of the headland at the end of the cove. The cycle path now takes you round the edge of the port, through the industrial estate and right, past the marina. You are shortly back at the ferry terminus.

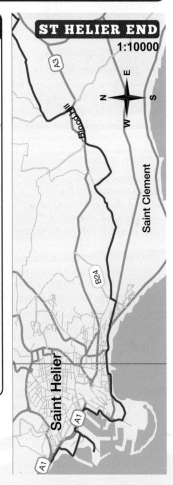

ST HELIER END
1:10000

Saint Clement

Saint Helier

CYCLING
NORTHERN
FRANCE
CYCLE ROUTES NORTH OF THE LOIRE

RICHARD PEACE & ANDREW STEVENSON

Done the Petit Tour de Manche and looking for more French routes to try?

CYCLING NORTHERN FRANCE

* Spiral bound 256 page guidebook & waterproof map package.
* 8 touring routes with 1:200,000 mapping, including the Avenue Verte (Dieppe-Paris) and a Seine valley 'return route' from Paris to Le Havre. Also features a Brittany Coast to Coast route and Around the Cotentin - and much, much more.
* Also covers all of Northern France's quality traffic-free trails.
* ISBN 9781901464283
* RRP £16.95

 (01924) 315147

www.excellentbooks.co.uk
richardpeace6@gmail.com

baytree
press

We publish guidebooks and websites to the most popular cycle routes. These include Britain's top three coast-to-coast rides, the Coast & Castles route from Newcastle to Edinburgh, and now the Petit Tour de Manche. For further details see: **www.cycle-guides.co.uk**.

All the best places to eat, sleep and drink plus up to the minute mapping and detailed route descriptions.

cycle guides

www.baytreepress.com